Best of WordServe Water Cooler / Book 1

EXCELLING AT THE CRAFT OF WRITING

101 Ideas to Move Your Prose to the Next Level

Compiled and Edited by Greg Johnson

FaithHappenings Publishers

Cover Design: ©Angela Bouma
Book Layout ©2013 BookDesignTemplates.com

Excelling at the Craft of Writing – 1st ed.
ISBN: Softcover: 978-1-941555-12-5

This book was printed in the United States of America.
To order additional copies of this book, or to inquire about permissions, contact: info@faithhappenings.com

FaithHappenings Publishers,
a division of FaithHappenings.com
7061 S. University Blvd., Suite 307 | Centennial, CO 80122

CONTENTS

Part II. Characterization and Dialogue

Part III. Plotting, Timing, and Structure

Part IV. Setting the Scene

Part V. Style, Language, and Voice

Part VI. Process

Part VIII. Pitching Your Work

Introduction

Writing is a bit like marriage.

If you're not reading at least a book or two a year about it, you'll likely fall into bad habits, old patterns . . . and you won't implement new ideas that could strengthen your skills.

The good news is that you've opened the right book if you're looking to get some great ideas to hone the quality of your writing. (Sorry, no marriage advice enclosed.)

As the president of WordServe Literary, a top literary agency, I'm pretty certain we can't sell a publisher on a bad book by someone with a great platform. But we have been known to place a great book by someone with little or no platform. And so for us, while platform and marketing are important, they don't seal the deal; even today, it's still mostly about the quality of your prose, the craft, and how well your book is written.

We want great writers! And, it turns out, so do publishers. Each year we sell about 15–20 new authors, many of them without a great platform.

When I go to a writer's conference, I'm looking for three things:

1. New writers with a fresh idea and/or a unique story.
2. New writers who understand they have to "come to play" and are willing to do what it takes to build their platform to help *us* help *them* get noticed by publishers.
3. But mostly, I'm looking for that one, perhaps two, great writers who wow me with their words on the

page. We can sometimes work with low-profile authors; we can find or add to great ideas or stories; but if someone doesn't make a splash with their prose, whether fiction or nonfiction, then we likely can't help them.

This book is all about ideas. While we boast "101 ideas" on the cover, the truth is, there are likely dozens more than that. They come from writers WordServe has represented over the years, in various stages of their publishing careers. All were originally posted on our award-winning blog, the WordServe Water Cooler (www.wordservewatercooler.com).

If you're already writing your first or perhaps even your tenth book, then there is no doubt you have some of the basics down. The chapters that follow are sure to give you ten, twenty, perhaps thirty NEW and SOLID ideas on how to make your work even better. There is value in these pages for writers at any level of skill and publishing history. If you implement even five or ten of the thirty great ideas that stand out to you, that may be enough to put you over the top to getting published.

If you're a novelist, this book is for you. A good portion of this book is specifically for fiction writers who must, must, *must* get better at their voice and craft.

If you're a nonfiction writer, there are plenty of great ideas for you on how to craft your book or your proposal and how to make your words zing so that your work can't be put down. And while some of the chapters are directed at novelists, don't think that you shouldn't read the advice given to them. After all, even nonfiction authors have to tell stories in their books to keep readers turning pages. There's a skill to storytelling, and you must get better at it!

xiv | BEST OF WORDSERVE WATER COOLER

So grab a pen if you bought this book in paper, and keep your highlighter finger handy if you have this book on e-book. You're going to want to mark these pages up.

And when you're ready to make your submission to an agent, keep www.wordserveliterary.com in mind. Everything gets a fair look. You just never know what might happen.

Greg Johnson
President, WordServe Literary Agency
Founder & CEO, FaithHappenings.com

I.

Nonfiction Essentials

ONE

Powerful Nonfiction Writing

Alice Crider

Keeping in mind that nonfiction readers invest their time and money in books that meet a felt need, a great philosophy is, "Offer them what they *want*, then give them what they *need*." Here are fourteen questions to consider as you write your life-changing message:

- What problem is your reader experiencing?
- How has the problem been overlooked?
- What are they missing out on due to this problem?
- What impact has this problem had on their life?
- What misconceptions has the reader bought into that might keep him/her from experiencing the benefit you're about to offer?
- What underlying beliefs do they have that keep them from seeing a new solution or alternate view?
- What solution or benefit will you show the reader?
- What truths will help the reader see the benefit?
- What will give them an "aha" moment?
- What might influence the reader to avoid possible change?
- How are others enjoying the benefit you're teaching?

1

- What will the reader let go of in order to adapt a new view of their life?
- What choice(s) will they make?
- What action(s) might they take?

Always keep your reader in mind. Offer them what they *want,* then give them what they *need.* As author Dean Merrill says, "Never stop asking 'what's in this manuscript for the reader?'"

TWO

The Secret to Page-Turning Nonfiction Writing

Anita Agers-Brooks

I couldn't take it anymore. It was driving me mad. Why were kids who chronically complained about their hatred of reading devouring these books?

Being the mission-minded gal I am, I decided to find out for myself. So I started reading the *Twilight* series by Stephenie Meyer. She grabbed me in the first two sentences.

"I'd never given much thought to how I would die—though I'd had reason enough in the last few months—but even if I had, I would not have imagined it like this. I stared without breathing across the long room, into the dark eyes of the hunter, and he looked pleasantly back at me."

Bam! She hooked me—and reeled me right in. A few short pages later, I knew Ms. Meyer's secret to writing for people who rarely read.

Next, I decided to go back and study another series that played the Pied Piper's flute to many a reader, young and mature, who previously stated their distaste for the written word. Sure enough, J.K. Rowling, of Harry Potter fame, used the same secret strategy as Stephenie Meyer. Both of their methods are right out in the open, even though they're hidden in mysterious passages. Rowling begins her first book with this intriguing statement.

"Mr. and Mrs. Dursley, of number four Privet Drive, were proud to say that they were perfectly normal, thank you very much."

Very different style from Meyer's, but effective all the same. So what is this magical thread both authors weave so carefully into their books? And how can we emulate the process without plagiarizing their work or voices?

It's easy. I've done it all the way through this post. Are you screaming at the screen yet? "Enough already, quit messing with my mind and tell me!"

Meyer and Rowling artfully created cliff-hangers in paragraph after paragraph, culminating in page-turning chapters. Some were so tiny they were nearly imperceptible, while others were breathtakingly obvious. There was no doubt: tapping into simple human curiosity accounted for the multitude of readers desperate for each new release these authors offered.

But both authors were also wise enough to provide the answers to the questions they created, while they simultaneously raised new inquisitive scenarios. They didn't leave the reader hanging too long.

And this made me realize: I can follow the same method while writing nonfiction. My style isn't the same. My genre is different. My content, theme, and messages are often polar opposite to the fictional creations of Meyer and Rowling, but I can still use human curiosity to my advantage.

Who says you can't build cliff-hangers into true tales and exposition? Look at Laura Hillenbrand's masterful biography, *Unbroken*, now a major motion picture. She hooked me when the first scene opened with blazing bullets and circling sharks.

I realized, the best authors of any genre tap into the powerful force that makes inquiring minds want to know. When a book gets slow, the author has failed to make us wait, or has made us wait so long we give up and move onto something else that satisfies our curiosity.

The answer to creating page-turning nonfiction is to use the element of anticipation to your advantage. And like me, consider starting your own *clandestine words list.* I've kept one for over two years now, where every intriguing word I hear, read, or think about is added. I used many in my latest book, *Getting Through What You Can't Get Over*, and plan to use even more as I continue to hone my craft as an author.

Here's the thing: whisper, allude, hint, or disguise—the secret hides in the use of secrets. This is an author's hidden weapon.

THREE

What My Students and I Learned this Semester in Creative Nonfiction Workshop

Patty Kirk

Big Thing #1: Neatening the messy truth never works.

<u>Story</u>: A sweet-hearted student wrote a moving essay about her difficulty with "being held" following her father's death. She began her essay with an amusingly awkward forced hug—an assignment from her Family Sexuality class to practice "hugging until relaxed"—and concluded with her "surrender" into her friend's arms at the hug's end. Everyone loved the essay except for its conclusion.

In a conference with the student after workshop, I explained what I thought was the problem: the resolution just wasn't as concrete and thus convincing as the wrenchingly funny opening scene. "Did this surrender really happen?" I asked. "It sounds like you're lying."

I didn't really mean to accuse her of lying, only to convince her of that disparity in concreteness. Turns out, though, she *had* lied—not intentionally, of course, or even with intent to deceive, but just to simplify the messiness of her struggle into a more satisfyingly redemptive conclusion. There'd been no surrender in that hug. After we both recovered from her surprising lie—as much to her as to me—she revised the piece to reveal what really happened, transforming a good essay into a publishable one.

Application: Tell the truth, don't prettify it.

Big Thing #2: Contrary to the usual creative writing mandate to "Show, don't tell," most good writing requires both.

Story: Two students who particularly explored this truth were a chemistry major and a woman from a missionary family in Kenya. Both wrote from a knowledge base completely foreign to us, thus running into a classic writerly problem that the missionary-kid characterized as "balancing explanation with story." Explain too much, and you end up with a boring commentary on what happened; explain too little, and readers get lost. As the chemistry major said, "The audience cannot read your mind."

Throughout the course, the students tugged at the delicate membrane between showing and telling, testing the delights and dangers of being too baffling or too, as I call it, "explainy." By semester's end, both consistently wowed us with their work, delighting us especially with a close-up of cozy Nairobi teatimes and a wacky book review/lab manual hybrid on the chemistry of poisons.

Application: To take us somewhere we've never been—which is, after all, every creative nonfiction writer's job—you need to show AND tell, judiciously.

Big Thing #3: Scheduled, specific assignments not only motivate idea-less students but—counter-intuitively—often result in their most creative work.

Story: Several students struggled with motivation and, as one put it, "finding something to write about" for the course's ten pieces. The first six assignments were pretty narrowly defined and came one right after the next; pretty much everyone found those fun, easy to write, and creatively empowering. Open assignments with longer deadlines were more challenging.

Application: If you're stuck, give yourself an assignment. And a due date.

Big Thing #4: Learning to write better teaches humility.

Story: Several students identified "taking criticism" as a struggle in the course of the semester. Here's a reflection from one student's revision account: "I was pretty judgmental of the big guy, so I tamed that part down. It felt mean when I looked at it again. I don't think I lost anything at all, the scene wasn't really about him anyway." The student's introspection and writerly focus say it all.

Application: Find yourself some honest readers, then pay attention to them. It'll help your writing and your soul.

Little Thing #1 (Big Thing #5): Clichés are like fungus: ubiquitous but strangely more embarrassing and disgusting than most other writerly ills.

Story: Student after student confessed to clichés. They hardly needed to, since I routinely point them out in class. Even their revisions had clichés—as do my own, unless I'm super vigilant. In class, I put quotation marks around their clichés in Google to convince them. The phrase "inextricably linked," for example, gets "about 715,000 results (0.15 seconds)."

In a way, clichés are wonderful: someone's once-creative, collectively approved wording. That said, clichés remain the bane of good writing—Oh no! That's "about 3,160 results (0.51 seconds.)"

<u>Application</u>: Look again. And again. They're there.

FOUR

When a Speaker Becomes a Writer

Laurie Short

When I was asked to contribute to the Wordserve blog, I immediately thought "*No.*" But almost immediately after the first immediately, something in my heart said "*Yes.*"

The truth is, compared to many other writers, I am under qualified, untrained and rather unconventional in the way I write. Particularly the way I use sentence fragments (and parenthesis) for effect. So the thought of having a lot of trained writers reading my stuff is, well, a bit nerve wracking. (If I was being honest it makes me want to pee my pants.)

However, it strikes me that I may be able to offer an angle on writing from a speaker-turned-writer's viewpoint that could be helpful. So with that in mind, I decided to jump in.

As far as some background on me, in my 30s, I published fourteen books under my maiden name of Polich. They were "How to" youth ministry books that sold like hotcakes in the audiences I served. However, just before I turned 50, I shifted out of youth ministry, survived a fiancé who broke our engagement to remarry his ex-wife, and experienced some new and deeper truths about God; and suddenly, I felt I had more in me to write.

I remember running the idea of moving from the "Youth Ministry" sector to the "Christian Life" sector by my publisher, who met me with the encouraging words, *"Good luck with that."*

I realized at that moment that switching book genres was not going to be done easily.

But I'm here to tell you it's not impossible.

By the grace of God, I got hooked up with a great agent (Greg Johnson), a great editor at Zondervan (John Sloan), and was contracted for my first Christian Life book, titled *Finding Faith in the Dark*. It was my maiden voyage, and it released in 2014. I am currently at work on my second book, tentatively titled *"When Changing Nothing Changes Everything"* (this time for IVP). It's due in three weeks, so I'll keep the rest of this blog short.

I thought I could offer a couple of insights from a speaker-turned-writer's viewpoint that might be helpful to you. Because when it comes right down to it, don't many of us do both? The fact is, in today's "Look at Me" world, holding an audience is a skill all of us need.

Here are three tips I've taken from my speaking into writing:

1. **Grab 'em in the first 3 minutes**

    There is a rule in speaking that if you don't grab the audience in the first three minutes, you have to work triple time to get them back. I think in today's world with writing, it may even be more true. *Your* audience can actually leave your book without you ever having to know, which is harder to do when you're speaking to them. (Unless they're teenagers and aren't polite enough to care.) Here's the point: In today's blog-reading, book-skimming culture, the first page of your book should be the one you focus on most.

2. **Anchor every truth you share**

No matter how great your point is, it will be lost if you don't break it up with something to anchor it. Whether you use an interesting story, a dash of humor, or a poignant quote, you need *something* to entice them to read on. In speaking, I call this *"Keep yourself from becoming boring."* I think in writing, it could be called the same.

3. **End with a pow**

    This may feel like too much pressure when combined with point #1, but there is nothing worse than a reader who has stayed with you till the end and gets rewarded with nothing but a re-emphasis of what you've already said. Surprise them. Leave them thinking. Say something new. Give them a parting gift.

How you *do* this of course *is* all up to you.

And one last thing . . . if YOU have a voice nudging you to write something that may be different than you've ever written before, Don't give up. There may be people out there who need what **you** have to write.

Capturing a Moment from the Past

Christina M. H. Powell

When writing my first nonfiction book, *Questioning Your Doubts: A Harvard PhD Explores Challenges to Faith* (InterVarsity Press, 2014), I added illustrations from my family's history going back several generations. My challenge as a writer was to capture a moment from the past for my readers in a way that enhanced the nonfiction content. Here are the steps I took to make the past come alive first in my memory and then in my manuscript:

1. Find an object or photo.

In preparation for writing an illustration based on a scene from the past, I gathered an object or photo from that time period to help me step back into time. I found that holding a tangible object from the past refreshed my memory and triggered the creative writing skills needed for storytelling in the midst of nonfiction content. Old crafts, jewelry, certificates, clothing accessories, or desk items worked well for me. If I did not have an item from the past, a similar present-day object functioned as a stand-in.

2. Involve all five senses.

We capture memories with all five senses, so we will recall the past better if we involve multiple senses. Listening to music from a past era, tasting food from an old recipe, or smelling flowers can help you remember an old event. Have your favorite snack, put a vase of flowers on your desk, and play some music, and then start writing!

3. Take a field trip.

If possible, go back to visit a place similar to the one in your manuscript. If you are writing about an event, attend a similar present-day event. Notice the details and the differences between the present event and the past one. Attending a university graduation ceremony as an alumna helped me describe my own doctoral graduation ceremony in my manuscript. To shape a scene set in the past, walk away from your desk to relive the memories.

4. Describe a moment in time.

If you are adding narrative material to a nonfiction manuscript, consider sharing a moment in time with your readers instead of a lengthy story. In order to better relate to my intended audience, I often chose a moment representative of daily life in a certain time period instead of a dramatic event or major milestone. By picking moments many people experience, you increase the likelihood of your writing connecting with readers. I tried to tell stories that hold truths that span generations and remain timeless.

5. Enjoy the writing process!

Writing down a tiny bit of history for a future generation of readers is a wonderful privilege. Relish the opportunity for a little time travel as you type the words of your manuscript. If you find happiness in your craft of writing, you increase the chance your readers will discover joy in the pages of your book. Smile as you take a snapshot of the past!

SIX

Five Ways to Add Humor to Your Writing

Dena Dyer

Humor is a life-giving stress reliever and ice breaker. I often sprinkle my talks, articles and books with funny word pictures and phrases, because laughter opens a reader/listener's heart to the serious points I want to make. Thankfully, my home is full of crazy guys (including my husband, who's the most hilarious person I've ever met) and I'm a ditzy, accident-prone bundle of midlife hormones. Thus, I'm never short on material.

It's true that humor, like writing, is an innate gift, and some people have it in abundance. Others…well, not so much. However, certain aspects of both crafts can be taught. Here are a few ways to humorously pump up your prose:

1. <u>Wordplay</u>.

Mae West said, "I used to be Snow White, but I drifted." Classic!

Cultivate your LOL quotient by reading children's books, which are full of marvelous wordplay. Humor writers and comedians are childlike spirits—playing constantly with sounds, alliteration, and rhyme. Let loose a little, and see what happens.

2. <u>Exaggeration</u>.

Never stop at one when fourteen will do. In humor, less is not more and more is better. Erma Bombeck, one of my all-time favorites, was a master at exaggeration: "I've exercised with women so thin that buzzards followed them to their cars."

Remember George Burns? He often exaggerated about his age: "When I was a boy the Dead Sea was alive."

3. <u>Surprise</u>.

When my nine-year-old saw that our local drive-in was up for sale, he said, "Mom, I'm sad about that. It's such an iconic part of our town." I laughed because I was surprised that he knew the word at all, let alone used it correctly.

Want your reader to laugh? Take a phrase and change the ending to something unexpected, like Jim Carrey did: "Behind every great man is a woman rolling her eyes." Stephen Wright makes a living by crafting surprise endings to one-liners: "A lot of people are afraid of heights. Not me, I'm afraid of widths."

4. <u>Parody</u>.

"Weird" Al Yankovich has been doing parody songs for years. More recently, Christian comedians Tim Hawkins ("Cletus, Take the Reel," etc.) and Anita Renfroe ("All the Wrinkled Ladies") have gotten into the act. There's even a clever parody of the infamous song "Blurred Lines" called "Church Signs." The writers make fun of Christians' tendency to preach mini-sermons with little plastic letters.

A word of caution (especially for Christian writers): let's be careful when poking fun at other people. Sarcasm can be soul-crushing, as can insult humor. Remember the Golden Rule.

5. <u>Learn from the best</u>.

Read funny writers, watch comedy videos on Netflix, take courses in humor writing, or read books about the craft. You can also hire professional humor writers to spice up your work (I did this with the first book proposal I sold, and learned a ton from the experience.)

While you're learning, though, remember to be yourself and not a copy of someone else. Readers can tell when you're trying to force a joke, and it will make them uncomfortable. Find a style of humor you like, and try it on for size. Ask for opinions from people you trust—if it doesn't fit, simply try another.

Most of all, have fun!

SEVEN

Four Tips for Writing About Sensitive Topics

J. Parker

I write about sex in marriage. Talk about a sensitive and potentially controversial topic. Even the idea of publicly discussing sex in Christian circles can trigger everything from raised eyebrows to scathing rebukes.

Yet I've always believed that if God is willing to bring up sensitive issues, so should His people. How can you address sensitive topics responsibly? Here are four quick tips.

1. It's not merely what you say, it's how you say it. Christians can be entirely right about the content of what they teach, and entirely wrong in how they treat others in getting their point across. Presenting truth doesn't excuse us from commands to be loving, kind, gentle, patient, and self-controlled.

Ask *how* you're presenting your points. Are you solely concerned about the issue, or do you consider the people affected? Do you invite conversation or lambaste anyone who doesn't agree?

If your readers see you as caring about them, they're far more likely to listen to what you have to say. Keep them in mind as you write.

2. Some react negatively because you poked a personal wound. Sometimes a reader's hostile reaction isn't personal. Rather, you unintentionally touched a raw wound.

For example, if I address how most husbands need the emotional connection of sex, I'll get angry reactions from higher-drive wives whose husbands don't seem to want sex, from wives whose husbands have been demanding or abusive, from husbands who've been refused for years and rant about how I'm too soft on wives, etc. Rather than feeling attacked, I try to show compassion for their difficult situation.

We should present our topic as fairly and lovingly as possible. But if someone freaks out about something you said, remember it may not be about you at all.

3. You don't owe anything to false teachers. We bloggers know these commenters as "trolls"—meaning people who troll the Internet for articles on a particular topic and leave comments that promote lies and hate. At first, I tried to engage these readers, but nowadays I can spot a troll, or false teacher, pretty quickly. And I don't put up with it.

It's not that a writer's skin isn't tough. Challenges, debates, and discussion are fine, but if someone promotes false teaching or personally attacks other readers, it's time to draw a line. Our readership relies on us to present truth and encouragement.

Adopt a comments policy explaining you'll delete remarks with egregiously wrong or dangerous teaching. Don't allow false teachers to soil your ministry by giving them a platform.

4. Find a supportive community. I cannot emphasize enough how important it is to find a community who'll support you when difficulties arise. My marriage author friends provide everything from encouragement to prayer to wisdom. And they laugh with me, which is healing in the face of trouble.

When it comes to writing, people who do what you do are not opponents; they are allies. Befriend them and gain strength from one another.

We can't dismiss our obligation to share God's Word boldly (Acts 4:31) and to help struggling people (Psalm 34:18) simply because it makes some in our midst uncomfortable. Your readers, many who'd never leave a comment or contact you, will appreciate your courage to address sensitive topics.

EIGHT

The Art of Bloodletting: Translating Suffering to the Shared Page

Leslie Leyland Fields

"The only books worth reading are books written in blood."
—Frederick Buechner

When suffering strikes, we are often silenced by pain. In such times, the act of writing may feel frivolous, exploitative, or irrelevant. Yet it is these dark, raw places of our lives that most demand our full attention, our most artful labors. We must steward the afflictions God has granted us. We may remain silent in the midst of it, but at some point we must write. Patricia Hampl reminds us of the responsibility that comes with our experiences: "We do not, after all, simply have experience; we are entrusted with it. We must do something—make something—with it. A story, we sense, is the only possible habitation for the burden of our witnessing."

Dan Allender, in *Forgetting to Remember: How We Run From Our Stories*, tells us what happens when we ignore the hard events in our lives: "Forgetting is a wager we all make on a daily basis and it exacts a terrible price. The price of forgetting is a life of repetition, an insincere way of relating, a loss of self." How then do we begin to write from within our afflictions? And how might the practice and the disciplines of writing offer a means of shaping our suffering into meaning for both writer and reader? Forgive the brevity and oversimplification, but here's what NOT to do and why:

1. Don't write to heal. Our therapeutic culture urges us to write into our pain as a means of self-healing. Newsweek's 2010 article, "Our Era of Dirty Laundry: Do Tell-All Memoirs Really Heal?" rightly questions this cultural assumption. I have mucked through some hours and days of writing that were hellish. Reliving an experience with language and full consciousness is sometimes worse than the original event. Recognize that writing into affliction brings its own affliction. And even more importantly, recognize that when we are predisposed to heal ourselves, we will not be fully honest in the writing. Healing will likely and eventually come, but only as we engage with the hardest truths.

2. Don't write to redeem, to turn inexplicable pain into sense and salvation. We want to bring beauty from ashes. We want to make suffering redemptive to prove its worth. But this is God's work, not ours. Our first responsibility is to be true to what was, to witness honestly to what happened. Our job is not to bring beauty out of suffering but to bring understanding out of suffering. Poet Alan Shapiro argues that ". . . the job of art is to generate beauty out of suffering, but in such a way that doesn't prettify or falsify the suffering."

3. Don't write for yourself alone. This is not just about you. You are working to translate suffering to the *shared* page. Buechner reminds us of the universality we should be striving for: ". . . all our stories are in the end one story, one vast story about being human, being together, being here. Does the story point beyond itself? Does it mean something? What is the truth of this interminable, sprawling story we all of us share? Either life is holy with meaning, or life doesn't mean a damn thing."

Writing can begin here, in the self, but should consciously move us beyond ourselves, to place our story into the larger stories around us, and ultimately, into the grand story that God is writing. The most powerful work comes from a "self that renders the world," as Hampl has said—not just the self that renders the self.

Life *is* holy with meaning. Pain *is* holy with meaning. Don't miss it. I pray for you the strength and faith and wisdom to begin to enter those hard places and to translate your suffering onto the pages we share—for the good of all, and for His glory.

NINE

How to Write a Nonfiction Book that Sells

Anita Agers-Brooks

You can have the greatest book idea in the world, but if it won't sell, what's the point in writing it? Unless you simply want to leave a legacy for your family and friends with no concern for sharing the message with anyone else.

As a Christian author, I'm driven to offer lasting hope to those who might read my words. So it's important I wisely choose the subjects, the titles, the content, the marketing plan, and the future books listed in my proposals. There's a lot I still don't know about this process, why some titles are purchased while others languish, but I've certainly picked up a few secrets. Some of them, I wish I'd known earlier. Maybe what I've learned will help someone else in the place I was a short time in the past.

The first and most important thing is to choose your subject(s) wisely. But with so many books in existence, and a plethora of authors scrambling for attention, how do you find a fresh subject to write about? Here's one of my secrets. I listen to others, but I also listen to myself. Both of my initial book titles came about that way. With *First Hired, Last Fired*, someone said to me, "Anyone can be replaced." I automatically replied, "Is that really true?" Voila, the subtitle, *How to Become Irreplaceable in Any Job*

Market, was born as Greg Johnson's variation from my first take on the idea of being irreplaceable at work. My second title happened when I heard myself say to someone, "You know, there are things in life we learn to get through, but no matter what anyone says, we just won't get over." A little tweaking and tightening later, *Getting Through What You Can't Get Over* became a book that a lot of people say they or someone else needs to read.

Listen to your own conversations. What scares us? What are we complaining about? What confuses us? What aha moments do we encounter and why? What works and what doesn't? How have we discovered hope and healing? For Christian authors, what does the Bible say that's relevant to 21st century issues, in the here and now?

The second most important thing is titling. I'd say the process you use to choose a topic works as well for picking a title. What grabs you? Can you turn a cliché upside down? Is there a pithy quote you can tweak to make your own and spread the message in your topic? What do you hear yourself and others say?

For subtitling, follow the advice of Alice Crider, my former coach and agent with WordServe: "Make a promise you can keep to the readers in every subtitle." Anytime someone offers us a solution to a big problem, we're interested. Right?

For this segment, I'd conclude with the power of valuable content. Slapping a few words together will not provide opportunities to grow your career as a professional author. Do your homework by reading books on writing well. Hone your craft constantly. Connect with other professionals and barter for editing/critiquing services; look for that rare mix of honesty and encouragement. Karen Barnes Jordan deserves credit for every book of mine that's sold. You can have the best concept in the world, but if you can't communicate it clearly, it's lost on potential readers and they will tune you out.

TEN

How to Craft for Your Crowd

Jan Dunlap

Audience.

Every writer knows that keeping the audience in mind is essential to effective writing: you don't include high tech specifications or advanced optical principles in a children's picture book about microscopes, just like you wouldn't fill your historical thriller fiction manuscript with footnotes citing the research behind your story.

But other than considering what your audience expects in style or format based on genre, how often do you start your writing project by putting the reader first, instead of the story you want to tell?

Over the last nine years (and eight books) as my writing career has developed, I've noticed a subtle shift in how I craft my writing. Whereas my first book—an exploration of Christian vocation—was the book I wanted to write covering what I'd learned from researching and reflecting on Scripture, I didn't understand how to make it compelling reading for my audience, even though I sincerely wanted to communicate my own enthusiasm on the topic with my readers and believed they would benefit from it.

Big surprise: even with a national publisher, the book did not do well. I needed to regroup, and start over by clearly defining my audience, and putting their need—be it entertainment, information, or inspiration—first. Only then could I take the story I wanted to write and frame it meaningfully for my readers, because if it didn't answer their need, they wouldn't read, no matter how much I wanted to share it.

I had to put others first. I began to pay more attention to what readers liked to read and why, rather than focusing on what stories I wanted to tell.

I applied that approach when I created my Birder Murder Mystery series. As a bird-lover and mystery fan myself, I knew there were no cozy mysteries about birdwatchers; I knew if I wanted to satisfy that audience, I'd have to weave together a specialized knowledge of birds, engaging characters that reflected the eccentric personalities who enjoy the sport, related issues of conservation, and accurate depictions of place. That meant I needed to do research to fill in the gaps of my own knowledge to craft stories that met those demands. Using that formula, I've written six books in the series and acquired a loyal readership that enjoys "virtual birding" with my protagonist.

Likewise, with my girl-meets-dog-and-finds-healing spiritual memoir, the first task I completed was examining my experience to identify how others could relate to and benefit from it. By putting the need of others first, it helped me organize the book's content: a blend of memoir, current research, spirituality, and humor. Otherwise, I may have written a straight narrative of how I learned to love our dog, which would be a nice story to share, but not unique enough to warrant publication.

The next time you sit down to start a writing project, ask yourself these questions first:

What does my audience need from me?

How can I be of service to my audience with this writing project?

How do those answers help me craft my content?

I think you'll find that putting others first is not only considerate, but a great way to write a book your audience will value.

ELEVEN

Memoir Writing: Scene, Summary, and Musing

Karen Jordan

What is a memoir? "I had to look up the definition of a memoir before I wrote my entry for this contest," one writer confessed to me.

"Congratulations!" I responded, acknowledging her award.

This writer's research paid off. Plus, she chose an inspiring, true story from her life, and she engaged her readers with a meaningful message using creative nonfiction techniques.

Being a judge of the contest entries, I also noticed that some of the other aspiring and experienced writers needed to do a little research before they wrote a memoir. So, I'm sharing here some of what I've learned as a memoirist.

My road to memoir writing started with enrolling in a class on writing for publication while in college. But I really didn't hear the term "memoir" much until I took nonfiction writing classes a decade later.

One of my favorite professors at the University of Arkansas at Little Rock, Dr. Sally Crisp, recommended a very helpful book on that subject by another writing teacher, Judith Barrington. Barrington describes her book, *Writing the Memoir*, as a "practical guide to the craft, the personal challenges, and ethical dilemmas of writing your true stories."

Defining memoir. Since I'm knee-deep in writing a memoir with my daughter Tara, I needed a refresher course. Here's my own memoir checklist.

- **Focused theme or topic**. William Zinsser discusses the memoir in his book *On Writing Well*. "Memoir isn't the summary of a life (like autobiography); it's a window into a life, very much like a photograph in its selective composition" (136).
- **Narrative**. Memoir tells a story about certain people, places, or events from the writer's personal life.
- **Reflection**. The writer's thoughts and beliefs about the events are a vital part of the memoir.
- **Conversation**. The narrative voice reflects on her thoughts and feelings in an intimate, conversational, and honest manner.

Creative Nonfiction. The memoir tells true stories using creative nonfiction techniques.

- Contains all the elements of fiction.
- Moves back and forth in time.
- Requires believable dialogue, based on truth.
- Switches from scene to summary to musing.

Scene, Summary, and Musing. Musing takes a vital role in the memoir. But scene and summary provide two useful ways to move through the narrative.

Judith Barrington describes the memoir's characteristics of scene and summary in cinematic terms. I've often used photographic terms to describe the editing process.

- **Summary**. Here the writer focuses on the panoramic view. This may include numerous details, but examines the person, place, or event from a distance. For this viewpoint, I imagine myself taking a photo of a sunset or sunrise over a lake with my long-distance camera lens.

- **Scene.** For this macroscopic view, you zoom in for a closer look at your story and focus on a particular point of view or incident. Consider using some dialogue to illustrate your scene or another descriptive device to describe an intimate detail of that moment. In photography, I change my lens and focus for a closer view of a child or the reflection over the lake.

- **Musing.** I visualize this characteristic of a memoir as the microscopic view, zooming in on the writer's intimate feelings and thoughts. The reflective voice of the writer expresses her feelings and thoughts at the time of the event. She might choose to express her current understanding or the wisdom that she gleaned from her personal experience. For instance, I love to capture the memories by the lake close to my home–the awesome sunrises and the poignant moments with my grandkids. It reminds me to record the stories that matter most to me as a gift for the next generation.

Storytelling. In memoir, the writer tells a true story from her life, using her best creative nonfiction skills. As you examine your memoir for revisions, focus on your areas of strength and weakness. Do you tend to focus on summarizing your story rather than zooming in on some important scenes? Have you reflected on what a certain person or event means to you or what you've learned from this experience?

I challenge you to work on the weaker elements of your memoir. Your story will become stronger and even more meaningful as you examine your scene, summary, and musing.

TWELVE

Want to Write a Memoir?
Read These Books . . .

Gillian Marchenko

Now that I've published my memoir, I've received a few inquiries about how I accomplished my goal.

Good question.

The genre of memoir is tricky. I worked on Sun Shine Down for four years and then spent another two years writing the book proposal, finding an agent, and landing a publisher.

Here are a few questions I get about writing memoir.

"I have a story to tell, but how do I get started?"

"What is your advice about writing?"

"Any words of wisdom regarding the publishing world?"

I am by no means an expert, but here is my best and most basic advice for those who want to write memoir (this goes for breaking into the publishing world as well because if your book isn't at its best, you won't break in): 1) Read a lot 2) Write a lot and 3) Find a class or a group of people to read and critique your work.

In this essay, I'd like to tackle my first piece of advice: read a lot. Here are three books every budding memoirist must read.

In *The Situation and the Story: The Art of Personal Narrative,* Vivian Gornick explains the art of writing personal narrative by reviewing key elements like the persona (or narrator) of the writer, her writing voice, and the importance of knowing who she is at the point of writing. The book is broken up into four parts: Intro, Personal Essay, Memoir, and Conclusion. Gornick draws examples from famous books and essays, explaining the situation and story of each, thus causing the reader to pause not only to appreciate beautiful words, but also to break down and understand what makes a memoir or essay sing.

"Every work of literature has both a situation and a story," Gornick writes. "The situation is the context or circumstance, sometimes the plot; the story is the emotional experience that preoccupies the writer: the insight, the wisdom, the thing one has come to say" (page 13).

My copy is covered in red notes and underlining. There is just so much good stuff in this book.

If you're not certain about the ins and outs of memoir, this book is for you. On the cover of *Writing the Memoir: From Truth to Art* by Judith Barrington, it states the book is "A practical guide to the craft, the personal challenges, and the ethical dilemmas of writing your true stories." My writing instructor at Story Studio Chicago, where I participated in an advanced memoir workshop for two years, uses this book with her beginners class. In my opinion, it is a book even the most seasoned writer can glean knowledge from. The table of contents includes chapters on finding form, dealing with the truth, writing about living people, and getting feedback on your work. It also has short writing exercises at the end of each chapter.

"Telling your truths — the difficult ones and the joyful ones and all the ones between — is a big part of what makes for good writing. It is also what brings you pleasure in the process of writing" (page 74).

If you write memoir or want to write memoir, this book must be in your library.

Handling the Truth: On the Writing of Memoir by Beth Kephart came out in 2013. This book is not so much about the 'how to' of memoir, but more about the value of the genre of memoir. It is broken up into four parts: Part I: Definitions, Preliminaries, and Cautions, Part II: Raw Material, Part III: Get Moving, and Part IV: Fake Not and Other Last Words.

"If you want to write memoir, you need to set caterwauling narcissism to the side. You need to soften your stance. You need to work through the explosives — anger, aggrandizement, injustice, misfortune, despair, fumes — towards mercy. Real memoirists, literary memoirists, don't justify behaviors, decisions, moods. They don't ladder themselves up — high, high, high — so as to look down upon the rest of us. Real memoirists open themselves to self-discovery and, in the process, make themselves vulnerable not just to the world but also to themselves" (page 8). See . . . you need to buy this book.

Attempting to write and publish a memoir is an arduous task. Start by writing, sharing your work, and reading these three books.

"Penetrating the familiar is by no means a given. On the contrary, it is hard, hard work" (page 9).

Right on, Vivian.

I would add that it is worth it, if you are up to the task.

THIRTEEN

Devotional Essentials, Part I

Paul Muckley

A well-written devotional can remind readers of key truths of the Christian faith, spur thinking that leads to a positive life change, actually draw people closer to God. A poorly written devotional? Well, God can use anything for His purposes . . . but let's consider some ways to "do devotionals right."

Just think how popular devotionals are—they comprise some of the best-selling and longest-lasting books in the Christian realm (for example, Charles Spurgeon's *Morning and Evening,* Oswald Chambers' *My Utmost for His Highest,* and Sarah Young's *Jesus Calling*), and they represent entire ministries (like Our Daily Bread, The Upper Room, and Living Faith). It's no exaggeration to say that new devotional material releases every single day, in books and magazines, on-line, and in outlets like church bulletins. How can we best meet the needs of this hungry readership?

I'd like to propose a **TEST** for you—that's **T**opic, **E**xample, **S**egue, **T**akeaway. Nail down these four elements, in this order, and you're on your way to an effective devotional reading. In the next two chapters, we'll consider each element in greater detail . . . but we'll wrap up this piece with an overview from my own experience.

My full-time job is editing books, but I've written or contributed to numerous devotional projects over the years. My most recent is *The Real Force—A 40-Day Devotional,* published by Worthy Inspired in Nashville. Here's how the TEST applies to it:

Topic: *Star Wars.* About a year and a half before the release of Episode VII: *The Force Awakens,* I envisioned a book drawing parallels between characters, events, and themes in the first six films to characters, events, and themes in Scripture. Happily, a publisher also caught that vision.

Example: Here's one of the forty in the book—the trash compactor scene of the very first film, later called Episode IV: *A New Hope.* I give a quick rundown of the rescue of Princess Leia from the Death Star, by Luke Skywalker, Han Solo, and Chewbacca. Escaping from Imperial stormtroopers, the four jump down what turns out to be a garbage chute, ending up in a dank, smelly mess far below . . . and shortly, the walls start closing in. It struck me as a metaphor for life: in a world that's already scary and dangerous, we sometimes end up in a really tight spot—and, frankly, it stinks.

Segue: Now we turn readers' attention to God's Word. In this case, I point out that three Bible characters—Shadrach, Meshach, and Abednego—found themselves in a similar situation. As Jewish men exiled in Babylon, they were already in a scary and dangerous place. And when they chose not to bow to Nebuchadnezzar's golden statue, they found themselves in a tight (actually a hot) spot, the "fiery furnace."

Takeaway: What does all of this mean to readers today? God saved the day for S, M & A, but He delivered them *through,* not *from,* the flames. I point out that Jesus himself hoped to avoid the pain of the cross (Luke 22:39–42), but "for the joy set before him he endured" (Hebrews 12:2), and that James wrote that "the testing of your faith produces perseverance" (James 1:3). Ultimately, readers walk away with some sympathy and some encouragement: "Tight spots aren't fun. Sometimes they stink. But God has reasons for them, and He'll always be right there with us."

FOURTEEN

Devotional Essentials, Part II

Paul Muckley

Devotionals come in many shapes and sizes. By "devotional," we might mean a single piece of writing, somewhere in the range of 200 to 1,000 words. Or we might mean an entire collection of such readings, perhaps in 30-, 40-, 60-, 90-, or 365-day packages. These details vary, but I suggest that the "devotional essentials" fall within the **TEST** described in the previous chapter. Here, we'll discuss the **T**opic and **E**xample of an effective devotional; next chapter, we'll wrap up with the **S**egue and **T**akeaway.

Topic: There are two ways to arrive at your topic: choose it yourself or have someone else choose it for you. That may not seem profound, but it is reality. If you want to contribute entries to anyone else's devotional project, you'll write to their topic—or if not a specific topic, to the general themes and style of the organization. Maybe a book publisher is planning a devotional for mothers of special needs children. Maybe a church denomination wants adventure-themed devotions for its men's magazine. Maybe your pastor is looking for devotions to go with his preaching series on family finance. If you're chosen to submit entries in a case like this, part of your work is already done.

If you're writing your own devotional, you have limitless opportunities for topics—though not necessarily limitless opportunities for readership. Sure, you *could* write devotionals that draw their points from thrash metal music, but you probably won't find a huge audience. Whether you publish traditionally, self-publish, or distribute your readings in other venues, you can address whatever topic is near and dear to your heart or whatever topic will help and encourage large numbers of readers. Ideally, both.

I have personally written full books of devotions on baseball (180 readings) and the *Star Wars* films (40 readings). I've also contributed to collections about movies in general, football, literature, the outdoors, fatherhood, and memorable Bible verses. Please note the focus of these collections—each book is centered on a clearly identifiable theme. If you're shopping a devotional book proposal, you'll probably get farther with a narrower theme (for example, running) than a collection addressing all your varied loves of running, coin collecting, *Seinfeld,* cats, and grand-parenting. Sometimes "all things to all people" is tough to market.

What do you most like to read, watch, create, collect, or do? Do you ever find your mind connecting aspects of your favorite activity with portions of scripture? Maybe that's your topic knocking.

Example: This is a micro version of your Topic, where you narrow the larger galaxy down to some individual stars. Say, for example, the Death Star.

In my Star Wars-themed devotional book *The Real Force,* I drew upon the Empire's fearsome space station for an entry about pride. If you've seen the original *Star Wars* film, you know that this metallic menace, in spite of its awesome size and power, did have a small vulnerability—a "thermal exhaust port" the rebels exploited to blow the whole thing out of the sky. The Death Star exemplifies a dangerous human tendency to shrug off temptation and the "little sins" that can blow our lives sky high (see Song of Solomon 2:15 and Proverbs 16:18).

Or take the larger galaxy of baseball, and narrow it down to some individual "stars"—like Babe Ruth and Hank Aaron, the original "Home Run Kings." Here's an example of success and achievement, and the human desire to be recognized as important . . . perhaps a king (or queen) of your chosen field. But no matter how far we rise, we're wise to remember One who is always and much higher, the "King of kings and Lord of lords" (Revelation 19:16).

It would seem, if your Topic is broad enough, that a little thought should yield plenty of Examples—ideally, with some related Scriptures (as noted above). Now, you need to put pen to paper, or fingers to keyboard, and actually start writing. Once you have a clear, concise, and compelling description of your particular example, the challenge becomes the Segue (transitioning from the example to the Scripture) and Takeaway (what you ultimately want your reader to learn/remember/do).

We'll talk about those next time. Until then, think about your favorite Topic and see what Examples (and Scriptures!) may come to mind.

FIFTEEN

Devotional Essentials, Part III

Paul Muckley

It's probably no exaggeration to say that millions of people—maybe even tens of millions—use devotionals as a regular part of their Christian walk. And while many of them are re-reading classic works like *My Utmost for His Highest, Morning and Evening,* or *The Real Force—A 40-Day Devotional* (sorry, just a little shameless self-promotion there), many others are looking for brand-new readings that speak to their particular interests or needs. Book and magazine publishers, web sites, and churches all regularly produce new devotional material for this large and hungry audience. If you're interested in writing devotionals, I hope you've found this "Devotional Essentials" series helpful. In this third installment, we conclude by discussing the **S** and **T** of the **TEST** I've suggested: Effective devotional pieces move from **T**opic to **E**xample to **S**egue to **T**akeaway.

While every aspect of a devotional is important, the **S**egue and **T**akeaway are truly vital. If your **T**opic intrigued someone enough to start reading, you've already won a small victory—there are plenty of other devotionals that she could have chosen. Assuming your **E**xamples are worthy of your **T**opic, the "story-line" of the devotional should keep his attention. But now we get to the devotional's raison d'être: the biblical tie-in and spiritual point of the whole thing. Done well, your devotional will educate, edify, even excite readers. Done poorly, it may convince readers not to come back.

A **S**egue is a transition, "made without pause or interruption," in Merriam-Webster's definition. How do we move from the **E**xample of our devotional—often a "secular" topic such as a sporting event, a movie scene, or some everyday experience—to the biblical teaching and the ultimate spiritual point, the **T**akeaway?

The **S**egue will be vary in complexity, depending on how closely the scriptural information parallels your example. If they're very close, you might not need any transition at all—the connection will be obvious enough. But in most cases, a **S**egue should bridge the two ideas. It might be as simple as inserting a phrase like "In a similar way. . ." Or the **S**egue may need to be developed over a couple sentences. (If you need more than that to explain the relationship, though, you might be trying to connect the wrong Scripture and story.)

Beware of the too-easy transition. In the "Home Run Kings" example of my last post, it would be easy (but cheesy) to come out of details about Babe Ruth and Hank Aaron by saying "And Jesus will always hit a home run for you!" Give your devotional more thought (and your reader more respect) by developing **S**egues that are less obvious and more memorable. While devotionals aren't a place for deep theological discussion, they can and should challenge readers with some fresh perspective on the Bible.

It's that Bible teaching that comprises the **T**akeaway, the point of information or call to action you want readers to remember. As with each part of a devotional, the Bible teaching must be concise—the **T**akeaway will challenge your skills of condensing material, while staying true to the actual context and teaching of your chosen Scripture. Ideally, the Takeaway ends with a pithy, memorable wrap-up that encapsulates the entire entry and sticks in the mind.

Let's finish today with a sample devotional that breaks out the elements of the **TEST** in context:

Topic: Major League Baseball

Example:

He was good enough to reach the major leagues, but not good enough to stay long. Yet he'll always be good enough in the record books.

Confused? It's a baseball riddle, of sorts.

The answer is Bill Goodenough, who appeared in 10 games for the 1893 St. Louis Cardinals. The 6-foot, 1-inch, 170-pound center fielder was a late-season call-up for the Cards, debuting on August 31 for a squad that would finish tenth in the twelve-team National League.

Goodenough's statistics were as mundane as his team's performance that year. In 31 at bats, he rapped only four singles and a double for a batting average of .161. He reached base six other times—equally divided between walks and hit by pitches—stole a pair of bases, and scored four runs. And then Bill Goodenough, apparently not good enough, disappeared from the major leagues.

Segue:

We might play off Mr. Goodenough's story to encourage people to try a little harder, live a little better, strive a little more to be "good enough" to please God. But that really misses the point.

Takeaway:

The apostle Paul wrote to Christians in Rome that "no one will be declared righteous in God's sight by the works of the law"

(Romans 3:20). Our good works aren't what please God—it's what we believe about the life, death, and resurrection of Jesus. As Paul asked the Galatians, "Did you receive the Spirit by the works of the law, or by believing what you heard?" (Galatians 3:2).

It's good to do good, but never think that's your ticket to heaven. Only faith in Jesus makes you "good enough."

Where, then, is boasting? It is excluded. Because of what law? The law that requires works? No, because of the law that requires faith. For we maintain that a person is justified by faith apart from the works of the law.

Romans 3:27–28

Thanks for reading. Now go write some devotionals!

SIXTEEN

Writing Effective Blog Posts

Jeff Calloway

I consider myself a Missionary Writer.

I began writing in 2004 with a blog titled, "The Southern Scribe." Even though I was an early adopter in the Christian blogging world, as time went on, I doubted that blogging was here to stay. Due to my time constraints, I gave up blogging. On occasion I would blog about something that interested me or blog about an issue that excited me or annoyed me. I can stand before you today and say I was wrong, in a big way. Blogs in many circles are just as pertinent as print and network and cable news outlets when it comes to breaking news or editorials.

Anyone can get an account on Blogger or setup a WordPress blog, but how do we write posts that are effective in delivering a message?

1. MAKE YOUR WRITING NEED BASED. When preparing to write, always start with the key need. Then move to the key thought or concept that has to do with that need. Be sure to research and then exegete your sources and prepare notes on your findings. Examine supplemental writings and books where necessary. A Missionary Writer does not write to be cool or famous; we write to lead people to changed lives. As I research, study, and prepare, I ask God for wisdom and direction.

2. EMPHASIZE SHOWING VERSUS TELLING. We should use current events and stories to illustrate the point we are trying to make. Remember, showing versus telling can get marred if we are not careful, as we want to tell people "how to" instead of showing them. The only way people really learn and are motivated to change is being shown how to go from point A to point B. People can only get to the next level by having someone who has accomplished what they seek to accomplish show them how.

Make sure you address the WHY behind the WHAT—why do people need to know this? How does it matter to their lives?

3. PROVIDE CLEAR ACTION STEPS. Effective writing leads to specific applications. In preparation of my writing, I always ask, "What do I want people to DO as a result of reading this?" In many cases, (calling for people to give their shoes off their feet), the action step may be bold. But in other cases, it could be simple (begin reading the Bible this week or go on a date with your spouse).

Just like meetings that do not include action steps tend to waste people's time, so does writing that does not call people to action. It's like running back a kickoff and stopping at the 10-yard line.

4. WRITE WITH PASSION AND AUTHENTICITY. Passionate and authentic writing begins from understanding one's personality and style. Writers that attempt to write like someone else will never connect as well.

In the 21st century, humor is a common language that conveys authenticity. People appreciate writers who do not look down on them, but engage them. Humor lowers people's defenses. Funny stories and statements can pepper your writing with spice and make it memorable.

5. BE SIMPLE. We often write about difficult subjects in an effort to answer people's questions, but do we use too many words without saying anything? Simple answers are often shorter answers. The attention span of our society is getting collectively shorter. This means that I must develop the skill to match the will.

Great writing should have one memorable point or statement that is repeated several times throughout the piece. There should be one driving idea, a "twitterable" big idea.

II.

Characterization
and Dialogue

SEVENTEEN

Five Essentials of Character Building

Michelle Griep

No matter the genre, every story has characters; otherwise you'd be writing a phone directory. Hold on. Bad analogy. I know plenty of characters in a phone book, and who in the wide, wide world of sports uses a phone book anymore anyway?

As I was saying, sans phone books, characters are an essential ingredient in a story recipe. There are lots of tricks to jazz up a character to make him memorable, but EVERY character needs some basic elements right from the get-go.

1. FEAR

What makes your character scream like a little girl? Centipedes? The IRS? The threat of an alien abduction and subsequent probe . . . wait a minute . . . I'm scaring myself. And that, my friends, is the point. *Everyone* is afraid of something, fictional or not. Identify what terrifies your character so that you can use that fear to ramp up the tension.

2. STRENGTH

I'm not talking six-pack abs here, though in the case of your hero, that's never a bad idea. What sweet skills does your character possess? Is he a crazy freak with nunchucks? Can she hit a raccoon in the eyeball from fifty yards away with a slingshot? Maybe this character has x-ray vision and can see into people's souls. Whatever. Give them something to work with. Even Charlie Brown excelled with his spirit of compassion.

3. FLAWS

Perfect characters make readers want to punch them in the head. Nobody is flawless, so make sure your character isn't either, even your super stud that swoops in to save the day and the damsel in distress all with one arm tied behind his back. This can be something as small as an inability to balance a checkbook, or feeding a gambling habit using stolen money copped from nuns. It's not mean to give your character a flaw. It's a necessity.

4. A SECRET

Psst. Hey buddy. Come over here and I'll whisper you some covert information because have I got something juicy to tell you! Are you leaning toward the screen? That's because you want to know what I've got hidden. Secrets are like big, juicy nightcrawlers wriggling on a hook, irresistible to the reader fish. Characters with secrets reel a reader in.

5. MOTIVATION

Everybody wants something. A brand-spanking-new Tesla. A mutton lettuce tomato sandwich. The stupid hangnail on your thumb to go away. Your character wants something as well. After you identify what it is, then dig a little deeper and find out *why* they want it. What drives them to go after their desire? That is motivation. I'm not saying you have to spell this out to a reader with a ton of backstory, but it's important for you as a writer to know because it will show up in their mannerisms and even in the way they speak to others. Motivation manifests in attitude. What kind of aura do you want your character to portray?

These are the building blocks of creating a memorable character, someone who will stick with a reader long after they've read the last page of your story.

EIGHTEEN

Finding the Fatal Flaw

Kariss Lynch

It is the core of every struggle. The root cause of many reactions. It is a constant enemy lurking below the surface, waiting to rear its ugly head.

It's the fatal flaw. Everyone has one. Every character has one, too.

I would argue that fatal flaws never completely go away. They just manifest in different ways as we grow and change and conquer certain circumstances. But what does this really look like?

Take Superman. I would say his emotional fatal flaw, or one of them, is a deep desire to belong. It shapes his decisions and actions to blend in at the Daily Planet, settle down with Lois Lane, but still seek the true identity of his parents. We all know his physical flaw is kryptonite. Or Lois Lane, depending on how you look at it.

Choosing and shaping a fatal flaw proved an interesting challenge as I finished out my *Heart of a Warrior* series. I noticed there are multiple factors I need to account for as I select flaws for my characters.

Timeline

All three of my books take place over the course of fifteen months, which made it a challenge to have a fatal flaw that never disappears but consistently morphs. Kaylan, my main character, struggles with fear. Since our fatal flaws never really go away, I had to figure out how to cause this kryptonite to reemerge as she grew. In *Shaken*, she fears letting people close to her because of the loss of people she loved in the Haiti earthquake. In *Shadowed*, she has to learn to love a man she could lose at any second, Navy SEAL Nick Carmichael. In *Surrendered*, she learns to accept Nick's career and the constant danger, and not only accept it but thrive in his absences. The root of every one of her struggles is fear of losing a loved one, but as she accepts growth, the flaw manifests differently.

Complementing Characters

If you are writing romance, what fatal flaw will most threaten the relationship and will cause the characters to have to fight together to overcome? In *Shadowed*, Nick struggles with anger and detachment. This creates a challenge when Kaylan needs reassurance in her fear and Nick needs her to get over it and let him deploy in peace. Both characters grow as they learn what it looks like to merge two lives into one.

Plot and Theme

Each book in this series had to capture the overall theme: Anyone can develop the heart of a warrior if they are willing to have courage and commitment in the face of insurmountable obstacles. My fatal flaw for each character needed to threaten accomplishing this goal. Kaylan's fear has the potential to stunt the relationship. Nick's anger prohibits him from being a strong leader in his home and confident and in control in war. My villain's flaw causes her to sabotage others in an effort to obtain what she secretly desires most but also never wants to have.

The fatal flaws is one of simplest yet most complex aspects of your character. Which flaws will create complicated conflict?

How does that flaw force your character to respond? How will your character grow through the flaw?

One of my favorite ways to identify character growth and a consistent flaw is to follow a specific television series. Over time, you will notice a core struggle emerge. This helps me understand how to develop a character over the course of a book and over the course of a series. I'm still learning, but this is becoming one of my favorite parts of creating characters.

NINETEEN

Give Your Characters a Life!

Jan Drexler

We've all been there.

You're sitting at your desk, fingers flying across your keyboard. Your hero and heroine are in the middle of a conflict and . . . wait. How does he react when she turns to walk away from him?

Every action our characters make is determined by their background. Their backstory.

Let's look at the hero in my September release from Love Inspired as an example.

Nate Colby is a Civil War veteran. He had been part of the Union Cavalry during the last couple years of the war. During one campaign, he was ordered to move a wagon load of explosives out of a burning barn. He hitched a team of mules to the wagon, but the mules balked. They refused to pull the wagon out of the barn.

The explosion nearly killed Nate, but more importantly, the experience was the beginning of a series of events that convinced him he lacks something in his makeup that other men possess. Something inside him causes him to fail every time he attempts something important.

It also caused him to hate and distrust mules.

Fast forward twelve years. During the intervening time Nate's view of his shortcomings has been reinforced over and over. His parents died while he and his brother were in the army. His sister disappeared into the west and became a prostitute. His brother's children were left orphans when Nate wasn't able to save his brother and sister-in-law from the house fire that killed them.

And his nephew's favorite friend is his pet mule, Loretta.

Now Nate is left with his nephew and nieces to care for, but the past still haunts him. It affects every move, every decision. And as the story progresses, the reader gets glimpses of Nate's backstory. It unfolds when it needs to in order to give Nate's character depth.

But Nate's backstory is so much more important than to make his character interesting to the reader.

Without knowing his backstory, I would be at a loss whenever he appears in a scene or when there is a plot twist.

For example, the heroine, Sarah, is a crusader, seeking to save the poor lost prostitutes in Deadwood. She is extremely naïve and idealistic at the beginning of the story, and enthusiastically recruits Nate to help her.

How does he respond? We—as readers—already know this part of Nate's backstory. Remember the sister who disappeared twelve years ago? Nate's experience with his sister gives him an insight into the life of a saloon girl that Sarah doesn't have. He not only keeps her enthusiasm grounded in reality, but he agrees to help her, even though he's afraid the plan is doomed if he has any part in it.

Nate's backstory drives his decision to help Sarah and his feelings about that decision. It affects all of his actions as they carry out Sarah's plans to help one of the soiled doves in the mining camp. And it provides the starting point for the change his character goes through in the course of the story.

Writing my character's backstory is a major part of getting to know my characters before I ever start writing my stories. It gives them life!

TWENTY

Thank You, Doctors

Jan Dunlap

I have a secret to share with you.

When I create characters for my novels, I often call on the expertise of two renowned psychologists. Their names are Carl Jung and Isabel Briggs Myers. Many of us know their work in the form of the theory of psychological typology, or the personality inventory called the Myers-Briggs Type Indicator (MBTI). I've found that once I start developing a character, I can turn to the Myers-Briggs personality types to fill out the outline of a character with true-to-life traits and behaviors using the four categories of personality type. In short, it's like a cheat sheet for character creation.

Let's look at an example using the first piece of the four-part MBTI.

I've got a rather demanding physicist I want to cast as my reluctant hero. As an academic, he fits the **Introvert (I)** type, rather than the **Extrovert (E)**: he prefers private time, doesn't do well in crowds, and is sometimes so wrapped up in his thoughts that he's oblivious to what's happening around him. I'd say that's a good description of a physicist who loves to work long hours in a research lab. However, since I want him to come across as blunt and insensitive, I'm going to throw in a little Extrovert: he tends to act first, and reflect later, in social situations he finds challenging.

Here's the scene I'm working on: After finishing a 20-hour stint in the lab, the physicist is awakened from a deep sleep by an insistent knocking at his front door.

Here's the question I have to answer as the author: Is he going to greet the visitor with a smile, because he can't wait to share the big discovery he made during that lab marathon? Or is he going to roll over and refuse to come to the door?

I decide he's going to roll over and pull the pillow over his head in true Introvert style.

But the knocking continues. He has to do something to make it stop because it's infringing on his solitude, which he craves.

Grudgingly, he drags himself out of bed; he's not going to be a happy camper when he opens that door. Nor does he want to talk with anyone (this is an awkward social situation, remember!), but because of that bit of Extrovert quality (act first, think later), he ends up jerking open the door. When he sees it's his least favorite colleague from work, he blurts out a rude, "What are you doing here?"

By using the MBTI as my guide, I've accomplished several things, such as giving him consistent character traits, motivation for his actions, and even the beginning of a conflict with another character.

By the time I identify the other three parts of his personality type—**Sensing (S)** or **Intuitive (N)**, **Thinking (T)** or **Feeling (F)**, **Judging (J)** or **Perceiving (P)**—I'll have the keys to his actions in any situation my plot throws at him.

TWENTY-ONE

Emotional Development of Characters

Rebecca L. Boschee

L
ast year I drew *The Emotional Development of Characters* as the topic for my speaking engagement at the Tucson Festival of Books. Part of me was delighted; developing characters is one of my favorite parts of writing. The other part was terrified. Character development, like many aspects of writing, is very individual to the writer, and while I knew how *I* did it, it wasn't exactly easy to explain, nor was I entirely convinced the majority of what I did wasn't done subconsciously. Still, I took the challenge and came up with a few pointers any writer might use as a starting point.

What do you remember most when you finish a really good novel? Are you left in awe at the amazing plot? Or do you have lingering thoughts about the characters? For most readers, it's the characters they identify with more than anything. That's because to care about what happens in a story the reader must care about its characters. So, how do you create characters your audience will care about?

One-time literary agent, now children's book author Nathan Bransford once tweeted: *In great novels, every character has their own set of goals, vices, and motivations and no one is purely good or evil.*

In other words, they are *human*. One way to make it easier to connect to your characters emotionally is to give them some flaw. After all, to err is human. You don't want to give them just any old flaw, though. It should be an important inner flaw, ideally one that plays off their strength. For instance, someone who is self-disciplined and organized (strength) may also be a control freak or inflexible (weakness). A strong and brave character (strength) may be overprotective and overbearing (weakness). Whatever the flaw, it should prevent the character from being the best they can be. It should get in the way of what they want, resulting in some internal struggle they will eventually face to overcome—or not if your story is a tragedy or the character in question a villain.

I like to think about my characters' strengths and flaws by getting a glimpse into their personality. There are lots of personality profiles available for a writer to tap into, but I use the Myers-Briggs Personality Assessment to sketch my characters' profiles. It suggests people have different ways of gaining energy (*Introversion or Extraversion*), being aware of information (*Sensing or Intuition*), coming to conclusions or decisions about that information (*Thinking or Feeling*), and ultimately dealing with the world around them (*Judging or Perceiving*).

If my heroine was Intuitive—trusting interrelationships, theories and future possibilities, her strength might be that she's aware of others, and she is able to weave together possibilities from bits of information. Her flaw may be that those possibilities are not always based in fact, and therefore she makes decisions using circumstantial evidence. Maybe my hero is Perceiving—adaptable and keeps options open as long as possible. While this allows him to be flexible and go with the flow (strength), it backfires when he adopts a 'wait and see' approach when he should be taking affirmative action (flaw).

Once I have my characters' personalities down, if I'm writing a romance I like to make the hero and heroine as opposite as possible. Those differences are ripe for emotional conflict. Or, maybe the conflict stems from the fact they are too much alike, such as Rhett Butler and Scarlett O'Hara from Gone with the Wind. Either way, the process of overcoming and resolving those conflicts requires emotional maturity if the couple ever hopes to be together—and that is one part of their emotional development.

Another tool the personality assessment provides me with is the framework for how my characters would realistically act in any given circumstance. You know that adage about sticks and stones breaking bones but words never hurting? It's a lie. Words hurt because they are aimed at emotions. How a character reacts (or doesn't) to internal and external conflict throughout your story should reflect who they are and where they are emotionally at that particular point in time. More importantly, it should develop as the story progresses, eventually cultivating in some notable change to the character's emotional self. Understanding your character's personality, their strength and flaws is a start to making their responses more believable.

TWENTY-TWO

How a Plot-First Writer Builds Characters

Erica Vetsch

I am a plot-first writer. My story ideas emerge when considering *events*, real and imagined, and only after all the events are in place do I try to figure characters. While my mind races happily along forming the plot, my brain comes to a standstill when it's time to zero in on a character to carry the story.

That is, until I found this handy-dandy little book: *The Complete Writer's Guide to Heroes & Heroines: Sixteen Master Archetypes* by Tami D. Cowden, Caro LaFever, and Sue Viders.

There are dozens of books on character-creation out there and lots of helpful resources online to aid in creating the perfect characters. I know because I've tried many of them. Most of these methods involve making endless lists and exploring everything in the character's past from shoe-size to perfume preference. For some authors this is vital to the writing process, but for me, it is tedious, boring, and keeps me from writing the story.

So I was happy to find a resource that was different. Here are a few of the things from *Sixteen Master Archetypes* that I found helpful:

With only eight Hero types and eight Heroine types, this book narrowed my initial character questions to only a few possible answers. Yet the types are broad enough to encompass lots of individual quirks while being distinct enough that your character will fall into a category quite easily.

There are multiple examples from books, TV, and movies to illustrate the different archetypes. I'm a visual person, and I love being able to pinpoint who my character is like from a pool of characters I already know. (Example, is your character a Free Spirit? Think Dharma from *Dharma & Greg* or Phoebe Buffay from *Friends*. Is your character a Professor-type? Think Sherlock Holmes or Columbo.)

This book gives examples of possible professions for each of the character types, as well as what in their history might've contributed to the people they've become.

And most valuable of all to a romance writer, this book gives examples of how the various heroes and heroines both clash and mesh, their points of conflict and their points of commonality, as well as how the characters change when forced to be together.

You might be worried that the choices are so narrow as to make all characters in that category seem the same, but consider this: Harry Potter and Mr. Spock are in the same category (Professor.) Thelma Dickenson from Thelma and Louise is in the same category as Dorothy Gale in The Wizard of Oz (Waif.) Plenty of room to maneuver there.

If you're like me, a plot-first novelist who has a rollicking story to tell but searches for just the right person to inflict all this conflict and disaster on, I encourage you to check out *The Complete Writer's Guide to Heroes & Heroines: Sixteen Master Archetypes*.

TWENTY-THREE

Jumping in the Deep End with Your Characters

Jan Drexler

Fiction writers write stories, and the best stories are the ones that bring the reader into the characters' lives. As writers, we want our characters to take on lives of their own, to seem real, to bring the reader along on the journey.

The best way to do that is to give our characters identifiable goals that move them from one end of the book to the other, propelling them forward until they reach their dream.

Sounds simple, right? Well, it isn't quite that simple.

Our hero doesn't just need a goal—the "what" of what he wants. We need to dig a little deeper. For example, your hero wants to become a doctor. That's a worthy goal. But what makes it an important goal, one that the readers care about, is that he wants to become a doctor because his younger brother died of a mysterious disease. He wants to identify the disease and find a cure for it. That's his motivation, the thing that keeps him moving toward his goal.

What keeps the reader turning the page, though, is that there is something or someone in conflict with the hero, trying to keep him from attaining his goal. Perhaps it's a lack of money that keeps him from going to school. Perhaps it's another medical student who competes with him at every turn – cheating whenever he can. Perhaps your hero has the same disease that killed his brother, and he knows he has a limited time to find the cure. Or maybe it's the hero's daughter who has the disease . . . that ramps up the tension a bit, doesn't it?

This concept is covered well in one of my favorite writing books, *Goal, Motivation and Conflict* by Debra Dixon. I try to read it at least once a year, and I learn a bit more about GMC every time I read it.

But I recently found something else to use to bring my readers deeper into my characters' lives. As we write, we often ask ourselves, "What would my hero do in this situation?" To go deeper, you need to know not only what your character would do, but what your character would *never* do.

Let's look at our hero who wants to be the doctor. He's smart, good-looking, dedicated, compassionate, honest. We know what he would do in most situations. We also know he would *never* murder anyone. How could he? He's dedicated his life to helping people.

But think how the tension would crackle if you put your doctor-to-be in a situation where he has to make a choice between the life of a stranger and the life of his daughter. What would he do? Could he do the unthinkable?

Taking your readers through your hero's thoughts and emotions as he wrestles with that decision brings them deeper into his character than anything else you can do. They sweat with him as he realizes he's in a no-win situation. They feel the dread of making a decision that will haunt him for the rest of his life. And they celebrate with him when he comes upon the only solution – the perfect solution that preserves both lives.

So think about the hero or heroine in your work in progress. What is the one thing he or she would never do?

And what situation will guarantee they'll have to contemplate taking that step?

TWENTY-FOUR

Knowing My Characters

Henry McLaughlin

The more I explore this writing stuff, the more I learn how much I don't know, or can do better.

I've recently come across two techniques that help me probe deeper into my main character and discover new things about her, new insights that add rich texture to her, to her relationships, and to the story.

In his book *Conflict & Suspense*, James Scott Bell writes, "The stakes in an emotionally satisfying novel have to be *death*." These include physical, professional, and psychological.

My current work is about a female attorney, Emily Peyton, in the 1880s. In the main conflict in the book, her first trial, she defends a man accused of murder. She faces both professional and psychological death. A conviction would mean she failed as an attorney and would damage, if not destroy, her confidence in her ability to practice the profession she loves. In her professional career, Emily must overcome the prejudices of a male-dominated world. To lose the trial would give credence to all those who say the law is no profession for a woman. A conviction also adds a burden of guilt over having her client face the gallows for a crime she believes he didn't commit.

Randy Ingermanson teaches the importance of our characters having internal conflicts. Such conflicts follow the character throughout the story and present emotional dilemmas she must overcome. These internal conflicts are identified through value statements, core beliefs that drive her. These beliefs are best identified through "Nothing is more important than . . ." sentences, such as:

Nothing is more important to Emily than being accepted as an attorney.

Nothing is more important to Emily than seeing justice prevail.

The internal conflict arises when these value statements collide. Emily's value of being accepted as an attorney conflicts with her value to see justice prevail when she risks her career to do all she can to have her client acquitted.

The keys to the value statements are they must be equally strong and, at some point in the story, they must come into conflict, forcing the character to make a choice.

TWENTY-FIVE

Self-Editing Tips: Character

Barbara Scott

In this post, let's concentrate on an aspect of self-editing that writers spend little or no time examining as they go through each successive draft of their novel: character. The people who populate a novel should seem real to the author, and yet, readers often notice that characters are stereotypes—cardboard cutouts.

To explain the importance of knowing your characters well, let me use an example from the relationship between the famous editor Maxwell Perkins and the well-known author F. Scott Fitzgerald, who wrote *The Great Gatsby*.

After reading the manuscript for *The Great Gatsby*, Perkins wrote a note to Fitzgerald about one of his characters, which read:

"Among a set of characters marvelously palpable and vital—I would know Tom Buchanan if I met him on the street and would avoid him—Gatsby is somewhat vague. The reader's eyes can never quite focus upon him, his outlines are dim. Now everything about Gatsby is more or less a mystery, i.e., more or less vague, and this may be somewhat of an artistic intention, but I think it is mistaken."

Every scene in your story should have an objective—a goal— but so should every character. Characters need motive. They must seem realistic in all they do, as though they truly exist—as if they live down the street.

Fitzgerald, no slacker when it came to building characters, reexamined Gatsby through the eyes of his famous editor and wrote a note back to Perkins:

"I myself didn't know what Gatsby looked like or was engaged in & you felt it. If I'd known & kept it from you you'd have been too impressed with my knowledge to protest. This is a complicated idea but I'm sure you'll understand. But I know now—and as a penalty for not having known first, in other words to make sure, I'm going to tell more."

To fulfill Gatsby's objective in the novel, Fitzgerald needed to make him a mysterious character, but to accomplish his purpose, the author also needed to know Gatsby's history to make him real.

A reader doesn't need to know who Gatsby's childhood enemy was, but if that relationship shaped his character, Fitzgerald as the author should know the backstory. Do you know your character's history, or did you begin your novel with only a vague sense of what kind of character needed to occupy a certain place in your plot?

My suggestion is to keep a journal or notebook or electronic file on every character, including photos (look for images online) and make notes throughout your writing journey on character development. Or some authors need visual cues instead and will put together a storyboard they can hang on a bulletin board nearby. As you self-edit, you can then look back at the record of your character's motives, history, tone of voice, and other details to make their dialogue and actions consistent and believable.

To make your characters come alive, remember they are more than the sum of their physical traits. Characters possess

social, psychological, emotional, and spiritual uniqueness as
well.

TWENTY-SIX

Plain, Ordinary, or Beautiful?

Dianne Christner

Once I made the mistake of creating a heroine who wasn't loveable because she didn't forgive until the end of the story. Although her black-and-white thinking was true to character in her particular setting, it made her unappealing to the modern, more open-minded reader. Some who couldn't relate blasted her in reviews.

Observation: Characters can be too realistic.

While she needs to stay true to her personality type, a good heroine breaks out of the norm for her particular setting from the get-go.

Because writing is a creative process, the rules are loose to allow us to create a unique voice. It's a painful process to learn what works through our failures. After a dozen novels, workshops, and self-help studying, I still blunder my way along. At the end of each novel, I find myself vowing, *Wow, I'll never do that again. No more prologues for me*—but that's a topic for another day.

Under deadline, I write and juggle life. But between contracts, I study, plot, fret, and find more time to doubt myself. As you might have guessed, I'm currently developing characters. While fretting over my next heroine, I asked myself, *what would help her connect with readers on page one and throughout my manuscript?* This thinking led to another observation. Let me explain.

Growing up as a Mennonite, I call myself a plain-vain gal.

I was raised on humble pie and continue to strive for humility. But you know how it goes when somebody says you can't have something. So if I'm honest, I have a craving for beauty and admiration. When I read, I enjoy living—escaping through beautiful, gutsy heroines. Most of my heroines have been lovely on the outside.

But since I'm wallowing in character fret-mode, I polled my Facebook followers with the following question:

Do you prefer a beautiful heroine or a plain one?

Every single response was **plain**, except for a few who didn't care. Really? I expected the comments about inner beauty, but I was shocked they demanded plain on the outside. I expected mixed preferences.

For sure, they want a heroine who overcomes the ordinary. I'm still processing this information so I ask you . . .

. . . Is inner beauty or character strength more visible on a plain heroine?

As an example, Katharine Hepburn comes to mind, and I did a follow-up blog post about using her as a character on *plain girl romanticizing*.

I'm conforming to my followers' preference. Like most authors, I cut photos for each character and study them as I write. I chose a plain-Jane photo for my WIP—and she's really growing on me. I'm convinced I'll make her shine. And hopefully make her smile too.

This got me thinking: What about our heroes? In secular romance novels, heroes are often dark and brooding with wicked pasts. It's up to the heroine to bring out the good and change him. In Christian novels, the growth is often attributed to God. But what kind of heroes are Christian women seeking?

From my own experience, my favorite hero was my last one. He was ordinary looking. On a scale of one to ten, he started below zero with the heroine, who remembered him as gawky and pesky from college. I developed his inner strength and found myself drawn to him more than my good-looking heroes.

On book covers, publishers often hide the heroine's face. But writers must describe character attributes.

TWENTY-SEVEN

The 'Real Stuff' of Character Building

Jan Dunlap

A few years ago, my sister gave me a t-shirt that reads, "Careful or you will end up in my novel." She meant it as a joke, but the truth is that my t-shirt does not lie: for me, every person I meet is a potential character in my mystery series. Like every writer, my writing is informed by my experiences and that includes experiences of people.

That said, none of my fictional characters are 'real.' Though they may be inspired by someone I meet, I usually take my creative license very seriously and make my characters composites of traits that fit the needs of my story lines. For example, I met a charming World War II veteran at a dinner speaking engagement last fall. He kept everyone at the table laughing with his wisecracks and his stories of being an ordnance (explosives expert) officer during his military career. When he noted that he still had all ten original fingers, I knew I had to use that line in a novel, so I began to formulate the character of Vern Metternick in my upcoming release.

What was even more surprising to me—and especially delightful!—was that as I developed the character and his relationships with other characters in the book, I realized his explosives experience could lead to a key, and very funny, scene in the novel that I had not anticipated. So my chance dinner partner unknowingly not only gave me the kernel for a wonderful character, but also actually helped shape the plot of the book. It really is true that authors can create characters, but not always control them, and I say that's a good thing! Especially when those characters can solve knotty plot problems and make the book even better than I had planned.

There is also a flip side to my t-shirt—on occasion, I do use real people in my mystery series. Since my books deal with current conservation issues, and I aim for strong local connections, I use real places in my books, and actual experts in the story. I always ask those folks for permission to write them into the novel and then thank them in my acknowledgments. To put them at ease, I promise not to make them murderers (unless they ask to be!), and I generally give them an overview of how they'll fit into the story. So far, no one has turned me down, and I get a real-life connection out of it that my readers love . . . not to mention one more person who is almost as excited as I am when the book debuts!

As a result, I assure my friends who see my shirt that their secrets are safe with me. Besides, they can always take comfort in that lovely disclaimer that prefaces fiction: "Any resemblance to actual events, locales, or persons, living or dead, is coincidental."

And if you believe that, I have some ocean-front property in Arizona I'd be happy to sell you.

TWENTY-EIGHT

Conflict: The Heart of Your Story

Jan Drexler

One consistent problem most writers—new or seasoned—have when they're developing their stories (present company included!) is to bring enough conflict into the story.

It's normal to want to protect our characters from conflict. We like these people. We want them to have happy lives.

But do you know what you get when you give your characters happy lives that are free from any conflict? That's right.

Boring fiction.

You need to bring conflict into their lives!

But how?

The first thing to remember is that conflict can be defined as goals that are blocked or defeated. So before you can have conflict, your character needs to have goals.

In my previous chapter "Jumping in the Deep End with Your Characters," I mentioned Debra Dixon's book, *Goals, Motivation and Conflict*. That's a great place to start learning to develop your character's GMC.

Conflict in the backstory

As I develop my characters' GMCs, I begin to discover their backstory. What happened in their past that is affecting them now?

For example, in the proposal I'm working on now, Samuel and Mary's story, Mary and her sister move from Holmes County, Ohio to Shipshewana, Indiana to live with their elderly great aunt. But why would they move away from home? What is at home that they want to get away from?

It has to be a conflict strong enough to force them to take this life-changing step. For Mary, it's a tragic event that happened to her two years earlier.

A conflict within the story for each character

So the next step is to find Mary's story conflict. I had to ask myself: What is the worst, the absolute worst thing that could happen to my character?

In my proposal, Mary's past tragic event is that she had been attacked by a man two years earlier, and since then the attacker has been threatening her and intimidating her–blackmailing her into keeping his secret.

So what is the absolute worst thing that could happen to Mary? That's right. Her attacker finds her in Indiana and starts the intimidation and threats all over again.

The story conflict is more powerful if it has ties to a past conflict in your character's life.

Of course, both characters need to have a conflict, so you need to do this exercise for both your hero and your heroine.

Let the conflict in your story increase toward the crescendo of the Final Battle

In my proposal, the hero, Samuel, is an alcoholic. He's fighting his addiction throughout the entire story. That's his first level of conflict.

His battle becomes much worse when he feels inadequate, threatened or guilty. When he sees Mary with her attacker, he assumes that they have a romantic relationship. That's the next level of conflict for him.

But when he finds out he's wrong and Mary is in danger from this man, he faces the "dark night of the soul," the Black Moment, and is on the verge of taking that drink he's been fighting throughout the story . . . and the conflict tension ramps up.

Your characters' individual conflicts work against each other, driving your hero and heroine apart

Ramping up the tension raises the stakes; the characters' relationship is in danger.

Samuel's alcoholism and feelings of inadequacy make him pull away from Mary just when she needs him most.

Mary's fear of revealing her secret—and of being close to any man—makes her pull away from him just when he needs her most.

I want my readers to question how these two can ever overcome their conflicts and have a happily-ever-after ending!

So the most important part of the story comes when the characters need to fight against this force that is driving them away from each other. The satisfying ending to the story comes when they triumphantly stand firm, fighting this final battle together.

TWENTY-NINE

Hero Worship

Michelle Griep

James Bond. Batman. Robin Hood. Every reader longs for a hero, and it's not just a girl thing. Men admire champions as well. This means that as a writer who wants to gain readership, creating a heroic protagonist isn't just a good idea.

It's crucial.

But what makes a great hero? Six-pack abs? Bulging biceps? A smile that makes every woman within a five-mile radius sit up and beg?

No. Even villains can look like Michelangelo's David can still be rotten to the core.

So, outward appearances aside, what goes in to writing a heart-stirring fella that makes you want to whip out some pom-poms and cheer until your throat burns?

I've given serious thought about the ultimate hero I can use for a model. King Arthur wins hands-down for chivalry, but Atticus Finch trumps with social justice. After much consideration, I finally came up with one all-time, can't-argue-with-this heroic figure . . .

Jesus.

I know. I know. To some it might seem sacrilegious to be so presumptuous as to try to create a fictional character based on the son of God. Far be it from me to think I can infuse divine qualities into a pen and ink creation.

But, hey, it's worth a shot. So here's a list of attributes to infuse superhuman memorable traits into your hero that will stir the heart of any reader.

Determination

This is the dude who never gives up. He's got a mission, and nothing will stop him from completing it. Readers admire a hero who takes hardships on the chin, all in the name of carrying out his responsibilities.

Strength

I'm not talking merely physical might. A hero must be able to withstand any number of blows, from mental to spiritual. Notice I didn't say he doesn't stumble or get hurt. Strength has an undertone of perseverance.

Compassion

A leading character must be able to look beyond an outward situation, zero in on the heart, then respond with love—even if it's tough love.

Defender

Any memorable hero is going to stick up for the underdog. There's a time and place for righteous anger over injustice, and this character is willing to take action to do something about it

Confident

Who doesn't admire a person that knows exactly who they are? Just remember, there's a razor-thin line between confidence and conceit.

Sacrificial

Giving for the good of others is an irresistible attribute that inspires awe and loyalty—not just from the other characters, but from your reader as well.

Those are just a few. I'm sure you can think of more. Obviously, there is only one, Jesus, so there's no way a 'real life' fictional character could embody all these traits and still be believable. Don't overdo it, and keep in mind that your hero still needs to have a flaw or two.

There you have it. Now that your character is super on the inside, go ahead . . . slap on some bulging biceps, and you're good to go.

THIRTY

Daring Dialogue

Jordyn Redwood

I have to confess that dialogue is one of my favorite things to write. It also is the easiest for me. Often times when I start a scene, I'll just lay out the dialogue first.

My love of dialogue likely stems from my real life job as a pediatric ER nurse. Communication in the ER is very quick and to the point. Cutting at times. There is little room for fluffing up someone's feathers emotionally when you're trying to save a life.

At the most recent ACFW conference in Indianapolis, I was fortunate to take James Scott Bell's class called Quantum Story where he touched on several different areas to take your novel to the next level. Jim is a great teacher and I highly recommend any of his classes or books on writing (of which there are many).

One area Jim discussed was his eight essentials of dialogue and I'm going to list them here. Remember, these come from a master teacher and storyteller and not little ole me who is still learning a lot about writing.

Good dialogue:

1. Is essential to the story. Fictional dialogue should never sound like "real life," where lots of mundane facts are often communicated. "Hi." "How are you?" "I'm fine—how are you?" It should communicate something inherently necessary to the story.

2. <u>It flows from one character to the other</u>.

3. <u>It should have conflict or tension</u>. There is the overall story conflict but then there is also microtension. I first heard this term from Donald Maass and he explains it as the tension among words, sentences, and paragraphs that propels the reader to keep turning pages.

4. <u>Just the right tone</u>.

5. <u>Just right for each character</u>. All your story peeps should not sound the same. How can you differentiate between them so the reader can identify them? The best example I've seen of this type of characterization is Barbara Kingsolver's *The Poisonwood Bible*. Each chapter is in a different character's POV but she's never obvious about it—like putting the character's name as a chapter heading (which I have seen done). The characterization/dialogue is so unique in differing POVs that you don't need extra help to identify the character.

6. <u>Unpredictable</u>.

7. <u>Compressed</u>. Characters shouldn't talk for paragraphs at length. Give the reader some white space as relief.

8. <u>There should be subtext</u>.

Here is one of my favorite exchanges in *Peril*, my latest medical thriller. The lead heroine, Morgan Adams, is not sure she's all that capable of holding onto this life. Her husband, Tyler, worries about her committing suicide and he's just come home and found a bloodied knife on the counter. This section occurs just after she's found alive.

"You can't scare me like that again. You are killing me with this thoughtlessness you have for your life."

"You found the knife?"

"Yes, I found it! And the blood dripping down the counter." He grabbed each of her hands and caressed his thumbs over her pulse points of uncut skin.

"It's not my blood."

"Then whose is it?"

"Our neighbor's."

"And if I ask her?"

"You don't believe me?"

He combed his fingers through his hair. *"Morgan, it's as if you're holding on to the cliff with one hand and lifting your fingers up one at a time."*

She brushed past him and headed into the master bedroom. *"I wouldn't have done anything today."*

And just like that, all the tightness in his chest returned.

This post first appeared on the ACFW blog.

THIRTY-ONE

Idiosyncrasies of the English Language

Michelle Griep

Don't panic. I'm not going all-out academic linguistics on you, but we need to take a moment to consider the quirks of the American English language (as opposed to British). More to the point: what is said vs. what is meant.

When I say: "Wow, that garbage can is full."

It means: "Get off your butt and lug out that Hefty bag, would ya?"

When my husband says: "Can I help with dinner?"

It means: "Have you been on Pinterest all day or what? Why isn't the food on the table yet?"

When the sales clerk says: "Have a nice day."

It means: "I don't care a rat's behind what kind of day you have as long as you fill out the survey on the bottom of the receipt and make me look good."

When words are spoken face to face, it's easier to decipher because of body language. But when the written word is your medium of choice, it's all the harder to convey what a character actually means. On the up side, this can be used to an author's advantage by choosing words that convey characterization via dialogue.

Or it can leave your reader scratching their head and relegating your book to the bottom of the stack on their nightstand.

What to do?

The best way to make each of your characters say what they really mean (and not give the reader a different expectation) is to know your character well before they speak. This requires some groundwork before you begin a new manuscript. Yes, this takes time, but in the long run it will pay off.

Know your characters. Know them well. Then use the words that flow out of their mouths to solidify who they are in your reader's mind. Those are the kind of characters that stick with a reader long after they've closed the book.

But Don't Overdo It

I love sarcasm. Give me a character who's snappy and snippy with their dialogue and bam—instant like-fest as far as I'm concerned. So it surprises me when my snarky personalities aren't always well loved. What's the deal?

Apparently I'm in the minority. Surprisingly, sarcasm doesn't head the list of likeable traits, which can work against an author while crafting characters. It is your job as a writer to make your reader fall in love with your characters . . . or at least want to have coffee with them.

THIRTY-TWO

Say What?—Writing Believable Dialogue

Megan DiMaria

Whether you write fiction or nonfiction, good dialogue is essential to the success of your work. Either the dialogue will draw the reader into the scene, or it will bore the reader—and as a result, she may choose to close your book without finishing it.

Know that good dialogue in books does not correlate to real-life speech. When you stop in the grocery store to have a few words with a neighbor the conversation is usually small talk. It doesn't have to mean much except that you value the person enough to spend a few minutes chatting. But in fiction (and in nonfiction), dialogue exists to enhance characterization, support the mood, convey emotion, and control the pace of the story.

The first rule of dialogue is to avoid dialogue ping-pong. People don't speak logically, and sometimes it's more effective to answer a statement or a question with a question.

The following examples illustrate dialogue ping-pong and interesting pull-you-into-the-story dialogue:

Suzanne slipped into the seat across from Angela. The cool vinyl chilled her thighs as she scooted to the middle of the booth.

"Thanks for joining me, Suzanne."

"You're welcome. How have you been?"

"I've been fine, thank you. And you?"

"I've been better, thanks."

Angela picked up the red menu. "What are you going to order?"

"I've heard the turkey sandwich is delicious."

***

Suzanne slipped into the seat across from Angela. The cool vinyl chilled her thighs as she scooted to the middle of the booth.

"Thanks for joining me, Suzanne."

"Did I have a choice?"

Angela slid the menu across the Formica table and flipped it open. "It was an absolute stroke of luck that I ran into Crystal at the flea market last weekend. If not, I would have never heard about your situation."

Suzanne gazed down at the greasy menu. "I may just order tea."

"I've heard the gazpacho is delicious." Angela cocked her head. "And like revenge, it's a dish best served cold."

Good dialogue develops and establishes characters. Characters need to speak differently from one another. Give your characters a verbal tic—"Ya, know." Have one character refer to dad as Dad and another call him Pops. Consider that characters may have different vocabularies with different people. A polished lawyer will speak one way in court, but when he goes home to the bayou, he'd speak differently.

Dialogue describes conflict, setting, and characters. Rather than writing, *Angela was the kind of woman you couldn't trust*, have one of your characters say, "Look out for Angela. That girl will stab you in the back and then accuse you of carrying a concealed weapon." Also consider that what is *not* said in dialogue is just as important as what is said.

Dialogue can control the pace of the story. To speed up the story, use short sentences with few action beats. This will give you a lot of white space on the page and create a feeling of fast motion. To slow down the pace of a story, put action beats, thoughts, or description into the story.

Avoid using dialogue as an information dump: *"Edward, I know you're sensitive about people questioning your motives because of that incident that happened to you in high school when the principal misunderstood why you were leaving the campus early."*

Dialogue is more than a way to express your character's words—it's a way to express the world you're inviting your readers to enter. And as long as you can write good dialogue, your chances of being published will increase!

III.

Plotting, Timing, and Structure

THIRTY-THREE

Writing with a Hook

Rachel Phifer

What will make your book fly off the shelves? A good story, high quality writing or a strong voice won't help you unless readers know your book exists. And for that, you need such an interesting premise that readers around the country are chatting up your book. In other words, you need a hook.

Yes, the dreaded hook word. I've heard about for years, but it seemed rather elusive. But recently, I've been studying my bookshelves to find some broad categories of hooks, and it's getting clearer. Here are a few concepts I've found.

Give beloved fairytales, historical figures, novels or paintings center or side stage. *The Beekeeper's Apprentice* (Sherlock Holmes), *While Beauty Slept* (Sleeping Beauty), *The Girl with a Pear Earring* (Vermeer's painting), *Dear Mr. Knightley* (a love for all things Jane Austen) and *The Constant Princess* (Henry VIII's first wife) are all examples. Readers want to spend time with favorite characters and art.

Tie the story together with a hobby. Ordinary hobbies such as knitting and cooking can certainly draw in readers who enjoy knitting or cooking themselves, but if you can find a twist, this will make it stand out from the crowd. For example, in *The Language of Flowers*, two characters with a love of gardening send each other messages not with notes, but with flowers, each delivery carrying a symbolic meaning only they understood.

Unique hobbies can give your story a little flash as well—i.e., custom shoe design or wild life rescue.

Allow readers to vicariously do something they've always wanted to do. I bought *Forgotten* because it was about a character who, after being stranded in Africa for several months, returns to find that her job, her romance and her apartment are all gone. She'll have to recreate her life. Spoiler alert: the book did not live up to its promise of the heroine of getting a life makeover, but that promise is what made me buy it. What other deep seated desires will connect you to readers?

Create zinger beginnings or zinger twists. When an old man in the prologue of *The Lost Wife* tells a wedding guest she looks familiar, and at last figures out that she was his wife just before the Nazis invaded Prague, that certainly sent readers to Amazon's checkout cart (me included). In *Half Brother,* a boy arrives home to find his mother holding a baby chimpanzee, and that's interesting enough to catch a reader's attention. Burying a zinger in the middle of the book is a harder sell, since it's not something readers will see when they browse. But if it's good enough, it can certainly get people talking about your book.

Start with vulnerable characters at risk. The little boy locked in the cupboard in *Sarah's Key* is a great example of this. But even more ordinary risks—a teen without adult love or support (*Dandelion Summer*) or a Puritan woman being coerced to marry a man she doesn't trust (*Love's Pursuit*)—are good draws. Readers only need to hear the concept to feel they need to see the character to safety.

Create a character the world depends on. High-stakes Tom Clancy-type novels where the character must stop nuclear bombs from detonating or bring an end to a plague outbreak, or fantasy novels where the hero/heroine holds the key to the coming war (*Lord of the Rings, Blue Sword*) are examples.

Begin the story with profound emotion readers can connect with. Remember, readers don't know the story or the characters yet, so it must be something they can easily connect with. In *Coldwater Revival*, the heroine is apparently stillborn at birth, but begins to breathe with the loving attention she receives from her father. In *If You Find Me*, a girl sees her father for the first time a decade after she was kidnapped.

Think about what made you pick up your last book, or even better, what had you chatting up the book to every reader you knew? Once you've found the quality that made it so compelling, you've probably found the hook.

THIRTY-FOUR

Amish Aliens Stole My Baby

Michelle Griep

Not really, but sure grabbed your attention, eh? And that's the point of this post.

Calm down. I hear you. You're a novel writer, not a journalist. Why should you care about catchy headlines? Isn't that a lame gimmick better left to the National Enquirer?

Actually, no.

Mastering the art of grabbing the reader's attention is a valuable skill every writer should hone.

In case you haven't noticed, the written word is exploding from one end of the spectrum to another, from e-books to self-published hard copies to blogs. Getting your work to stand out from the crowd is more important than ever.

Which begs the question: How does one grab a reader by the throat? There are many ways, but here are a few to toss into your writerly toolbox:

Shock and Awe

This is one of the tactics I employed with my blog post title. Think controversial. Think stunning. Think outside the box. This method is most often used by rabble-rousers who get a secret thrill out of rattling cages.

Warm Fuzzies

If you start off with something everyone can relate to on an emotional level, you'll draw in the human side of the reader. It's a pull that's hard to resist. In my example, I tossed in the word baby. Emotions are what set us apart from the rest of the mammals. Well, that and opposable thumbs.

Trendy Tidbit

The ol' *People* magazine approach, naming what's hip or what's not. Naturally this works better for contemporaries than historicals . . . but not always. Amish is a buzzword right now, which is why I chose it for my post title.

Opposites Attract

Jumbo shrimp. Government intelligence. Amish aliens. Put two incongruous words together, and if they're not cliché, people will sit up and take notice.

Now then, where to employ these attention grabbing strategies? Obviously your entire manuscript can't be outrageously intense. You'd burn out your brain and your reader would gasp for air. Nevertheless, there are key areas that require some eye-popping fancy footwork. These are:

- The first sentence of a book . . . better yet, make that the first sentence of every chapter.
- The last sentence of each chapter. Force your reader to turn the page.
- Back cover copy. Often this is where you reel 'em in or break the deal.
- The one-liner that sums up your entire novel.

So go ahead. Give this a whirl. Don't be afraid to stand out from the crowd, especially when it comes to your writing. Hopefully you'll attract the attention of an editor, not an Amish Alien.

THIRTY-FIVE

Pacing in Writing

Janalyn Voigt

When I was a child, a piano teacher let me play to my heart's content without worrying about such details as tempo and timing. I'm pretty sure that wasn't the best approach, which may be why those lessons were short-lived. It wasn't until adulthood, when I studied vocal music, that I learned to pace myself.

Pacing, whether in music or writing, is one of the methods by which we organize the creative flow. Order prevents these creative expressions from falling flat and helps improve their impact.

What is Story Pacing?

It took me a while to understand the concept of pacing in fiction, but relating it to what I already knew about music made it easier. Basically, two elements of pacing work together within a story.

Every piece of music has a tempo, or base speed dictated by the type of music and its mood. This is also true in fiction. A sweet romance will have a slower overall speed than a thriller, for example. Knowing the right tempo for your story is an important but often overlooked consideration in pacing it correctly.

Your story plays out relative to its tempo, which means that the slowest scene in a lavish historical epic, for example, will be much slower than the slowest scene in a mystery novel, even though both may follow the same story pacing dynamics.

Vocalists are taught to hold back a little in the beginning of a song so that there will be room to crescendo later. In a story, the first scenes introduce the main characters, set up the conflict, and hook the reader.

As your story progresses, scenes ebb and flow at a slower, then faster, pace. This rhythm repeats, and as it does, the time between conflicts decreases. This builds tension leading up to the climactic scene.

The story then slows and, like music, resolves by returning to its tonal center. In the case of music, that is the first note of the scale. In fiction, there is usually a reference or some sort of return to the beginning of the story.

How to Speed Story Pacing

I'll focus here on ways to speed story pacing, since that's where most writers need help. However, many of these tips can be turned around to create the inverse effect.

Tension: Nothing propels a story along like wondering if the heroine is going to make it to the station before the love of her life leaves town forever. Or maybe your hero is being pursued by a gang with a vendetta. These are dramatic examples, but tension can be created more simply, as when Rhett Butler reveals he has overheard Scarlett's declaration of love for Ashley Wilkes.

Unanswered questions create tension in these situations. What will happen when the heroine gets to the station? Will the hero escape with his life? Will Rhett keep the secret of Scarlett's love for Ashley?

Action: Show, rather than tell, the story's action in scenes written with minimal description, using a few details to evoke the setting. This is also not the place for introspection or thinking by your characters. Eliminate anything that would distract from the main action.

Dialogue: Because dialogue can be read quickly, it moves a scene along. To speed pacing, eliminate all extraneous tags and beats. Use conflict rather than agreement to give dialogue vitality.

Word Choice: Using short, snappy words will usually help you pick up the pace in a scene. Reserve longer words for those places where you want to slow pacing to allow the reader a moment to breathe.

Sentence Length: Remember that the more complex a sentence structure you use, the more time it takes for the reader to decipher your meaning. That's fine in slower scenes, but use shorter sentences, which are more easily digested, in places where you want to pick up the pace.

Scene Length: A series of quick scenes can often move the pacing along better than one longer scene. You don't want to chop things up too much, but this is a technique to keep in mind for the right application.

Chapter Length: Shorter chapters tend to be cleaner and more concise, which makes them more easily digested. They also act to quicken the pace by giving the reader a feeling of progress through the story.

Mastering Story Pacing

Learning to pace the stories you write isn't easy. In fact, it's one of the most difficult skills in writing fiction. Even if pacing doesn't come naturally for you, keep working at it and you'll improve. For a model that will help you plot and pace a novel, read "Plotting a Novel in Three Acts" and the related posts at my Live Write Breathe website for writers (www.livewritebreathe.com).

THIRTY-SIX

Six Subtle Ways to Increase Tension in Your Writing

Rachel Phifer

If you've studied the craft of writing for long, you know about tension. I'm assuming you've got adequate conflict in your story, that your characters have inner and outer stakes that are deeply personal, and that your story keeps the resolution out of reach until the last chapter.

But there are more subtle ways to keep tension in your work as well. Sometimes all it takes is an added word or a deleted sentence.

What to Put into Your Story:

1) *Increase the volume.* This is a term from agent and writer Donald Maass. With a single motion, word, or metaphor, you can make your scene more dramatic. Even a mundane task like packing becomes more important when the character does it with a <u>slow hand</u> or a <u>furtive glance out the window</u>. The reader experiences the character's conflict over leaving right along with her. Linda Nichols in *At the Scent of Water* describes her character's old grief as a wild animal prowling in its cage. That one metaphor revises ordinary grief into perilous grief.

2) *Break a victory into several steps.* Suzanne Collins is a master at this. Katniss in *The Hunger Games* doesn't destroy the careers'

food stash in one quick movement. She works out that it must be done, she distracts the guards from the food, she puzzles out how to destroy it, and then does it not with one arrow, but with three separate shots. The reader is left breathless as she tries to solve the dilemma with Katniss and as the dangerous action is drawn out, page by page, step by step.

3) *Write a scene that underscores the character's arc.* After you've written your first draft and have done some editing, you now have a richer understanding of what drives your character and what holds him back. Write a fresh scene that encapsulates this as no other scene has. It may just be one of your most powerful scenes, because it will demonstrate your deeper understanding of the tension between your stakes and your conflict.

What to Leave out of Your Story:

1) *Don't use inner dialogue that hints at what your character will do next.* My critique partner, Christine Lindsay, in her novel *Veiled at Midnight*, wrote a scene in which her character realizes that what happens next is up to her and God alone, so when she changes course it's no surprise to the reader. When Christine rewrote it, she dropped the inner dialogue. The character without any preamble looks at the man pointing a rifle at the stranger, places her hand on the gun, and lowers it. Because all of the drama is concentrated in the action, it's startling to the reader and the scene has more impact.

2) *Don't repeat yourself.* It's so tempting. You want the reader to understand your character's predicament, so you put clues into their dialogue, their actions, their inner thoughts, maybe even in other characters' thoughts about them. Don't do it. It slows the story down and reduces the tension. Trust your reader to get it the first time.

3) *Don't always have characters say what they mean.* Have your characters intentionally misdirect dialogue, respond to an unspoken question rather than the spoken one, or let physical cues do the talking for them. It's called subtexting. When the reader sees that the character has something to hide or that something deeper is going on than the actual words convey, their attention perks up.

THIRTY-SEVEN

A Matter of Time, Part I

Jan Dunlap

Timing is everything.

This phrase appears frequently in the books of my mystery series, because my protagonist is a birder, and the timing of nature determines what birds he might see in each adventure: depending on the season, only certain birds are (typically) in a particular area. The phrase also is a descriptor of a 'perfect' crime—timing is everything if you're going to get away with murder.

As it happens, *'timing is everything'* holds true for all kinds of genres, fiction and nonfiction alike, both in regards to content and the pacing of narrative. In this chapter, we'll take a look at how content benefits from timing; in the next chapter, we'll focus on the art of pacing.

Content is dependent on the context of your experience of time. Everything a writer writes reflects his or her unique perspective and experience of life. For example, five years ago, I could convincingly set a book in a high school because I worked in a high school, and the students and faculty I met provided me with the raw material for characters and plots; a year earlier, I would have been inept handling the same material. The take-away: no matter the genre, *write out of your own experience, because authenticity depends on reality.* That's not to say you can't write a medieval romance—you can research the historical details that make the setting accurate, but you need to infuse your own feelings and insights, based on your own experience, to make the story ring true. Pay attention to what's going on in your life, because that's where your story will ultimately come from—the feelings and ideas you have in response to real-time life.

Content is strengthened by its connection to what is happening in the world right now. The obvious example is the spate of books that are published when an anniversary comes around, such as the books that hit the in November 2013 to remember the JFK assassination. Holiday books do the same thing—they capitalize on timing. Any time you can connect your content to current events or trends, you accomplish two things: you strengthen your content by association, and you build in marketing opportunities. Are you writing a novel about a young person struggling to achieve success? Use current research about how depression can manifest in video game addiction to add intriguing layers to one of the characters; if you're writing a study about age 30 being the new 18, that same research would add depth and attract readers.

If you're lucky, **time can even solve writing problems**! I had that experience with my book *A Murder of Crows*, which dealt with the conflict between wind energy development and bird advocates. Mid-way through writing my manuscript, that exact conflict erupted in a neighboring county, furnishing me with ideas and even plot twists I hadn't considered. I don't routinely plan on serendipity to help me out with manuscript issues, but the timing couldn't have been better for that one.

THIRTY-EIGHT

A Matter of Time, Part II

Jan Dunlap

Previously, we looked at how content benefits from timing. Here, we'll explore timing within writing—the art of pacing narrative.

Pacing is what keeps your reader reading. In suspense/mystery/thrillers, pacing is easy to identify: what starts out as a problem grows steadily (and generally, rapidly) worse. When I write my humorous mysteries, I use humor to relieve some of that growing tension in my mysteries, and my uphill roller coaster ride is one of short climbs and plateaus; thriller writers often choose steeper climbs with no reprieves before the final sheer drop. As the writer, you need to choose what effect you want to create in your reader, and then manipulate your scenes and character development accordingly.

Note, however, that I didn't say 'narrative of story' in my opening paragraph. That's because nonfiction benefits just as much from effective pacing as does fiction. Think for a moment about the biographies, how-tos, memoirs, travel pieces, or any other nonfiction you've read recently. Did they keep your attention? Did the author tease you with promises of solutions or details and then slowly reveal them, building momentum so that you couldn't put it down? Or did you plod through pages of dry facts and lose interest to the point of feeling like the reading was a chore?

That's the tipping point for me as a writer, whether I'm penning fiction or nonfiction: losing interest. Even when I'm the one doing the writing, I try to think like my reader.

Am I getting bored with a litany of facts? Then **break it up**. Focus on one fact and bring it to life with a concrete, preferably colorful, example, then note the other facts briskly. For instance, in my memoir *Saved by Gracie*, I list items not to do with a new puppy. I got bored with listing the list, so I described how I totally did the wrong thing with our dog concerning the first point, then simply noted the remaining ones. Making a list personal will engage your reader and create momentum to continue reading.

Use dialogue. Even if it's imaginary, it can help your reader place themselves in the same situation.

Use a metaphor or simile to make your explanation more understandable. Details enrich writing of every kind.

Keep focus. Confine paragraphs to one point, then move on—visual cues like breaking up text help your reader follow your organization and your pace of developing thought. You don't want your reader lost in the middle of a page-long paragraph, because they might decide it's not worth finding their way out.

In fact, write your nonfiction like you're telling a story with its own beginning, middle, and end, and you might hear that awesome compliment: "It was such a good book, I couldn't put it down, even though it was nonfiction."

Timing really is everything.

THIRTY-NINE

Having Problems with Your Plot?

Henry McLaughlin

P lot problems?

Here is a tool that may prove helpful. Steven James presented this material at an intensive novel writing retreat I attended.

Whether you're an outliner or an organic author, these simple yet intriguing questions will get your creative juices flowing.

The questions open doors into areas of our story we may not have explored before and will lead us to more compelling stories.

What would this character naturally do in this situation?

Believability is the first priority. If our character does something he would not naturally do, it will the strain the reader's investment in him and in our story.

For example, say our character is an inspector with the National Transportation Safety Board. What's the first thing he would do at the scene of a plane crash? Would he ask where is the nearest Starbucks? Or would he ask if the black box has been found or if there are any survivors?

EXCELLING AT THE CRAFT OF WRITING | 113

Or, he's an ER doctor and the paramedics have brought in a victim of a gunshot wound. Would he ask when the next available tee time is? Or, would he assess the patient's need for immediate surgery?

If the reader notices our character is acting unbelievably, another character must also notice it and comment on it. Otherwise, our story loses credibility.

How can I make things worse?

Escalate the tension by throwing more obstacles at our character. Increase the tension to keep the reader interested. It has to be believable.

Say my story involves terrorists taking over a nuclear power plant and holding the staff hostage. How can I make things worse? Here are some examples:

They strap bombs to the core.

There is a group of school kids there on a field trip.

They start killing the hostages.

The daughter of the chief government negotiator works at the plant.

She's aiding the terrorists.

The key is to avoid coincidence because this will destroy believability. Everything must build on something that happened before.

How can I end this in a way that's unexpected and inevitable?

Readers don't want endings to come out of nowhere. The ending needs to be natural and inherent to the story. We want the reader to be surprised and satisfied.

In my novel, *Journey to Riverbend*, I established throughout the novel that my protagonist believed he killed his father and that he would never kill again. At the end of the story, I put him in the position where, to save someone, he has to kill the villain. The ending was inevitable yet surprising and satisfying to the readers. It was also believable because of the foreshadowing I layered in.

Steven James writes, "The first question will help focus your believability. The second will keep it escalating toward an un-forgettable climax. The third will help build your story, scene by twisting, turning scene."

FORTY

How to Tell Subplots from Plot Bunnies

Janalyn Voigt

As a child, did you blow bubbles? If so, you already understand something about subplots.

What does blowing bubbles have to do with subplots, you ask? Simply this: When you blew too hard, you burst the bubbles as they formed. Blowing too lightly, while it showed you there were bubbles to be made, didn't produce them. Only by exerting the right amount of force could you blow bubbles.

Subplots are a lot like bubbles. If you try too hard to produce them, they evaporate. However, they won't necessarily form without your help.

What's a Subplot?

It's easy to become confused when thinking about subplots, so let's start with a definition. A subplot is a secondary plot that complements your main plot. Adding subplots to your novel will give it layers of substance and effectively underline your theme. Layering with subplots adds texture to your story's weave. Good subplots form and grow as you write. Most show up early but can also make their appearance partway through a story. Watch for them as you introduce new characters or new situations. They can show up as a romantic interest, a character from the past, an obstacle to be overcome, or a past experience which is revealed over the course of the book, to name a few occurrences.

Most people would agree that the novel *Gone with the Wind* tells the epic romance of Scarlett O'Hara and Rhett Butler. Scarlett's relationship with Melanie Wilkes, her father's fate, and her relationship with her sister, Sue Ellen, are all subplots. Each forms its own story within a story, and yet each contributes to the greater story by shaping our opinions about Scarlett. None of these subplots is forced. Each arises naturally from the main plot and helps develop the theme.

What's a Bunny Trail?

It's sometimes hard to detect bunny trails. They can sneak into your story as a romantic interest, a character from the past, or an obstacle to be overcome. Like Pegasus and his brother, Chrysaor, they can spring fully-grown out of your backstory. Subplots should never lead the reader away from your theme and should, in fact, support your primary plot. A subplot happens *because of* (rather than *instead of*) the main story. Anything else is a distraction. It's true that all sorts of unrelated events tangle together in real life, but good fiction doesn't suffer from such snarls and is carefully constructed to represent, rather than emulate, real life. Understanding this difference is crucial.

Adding Subplots to Your Novel

As you develop your novel, give some thought to what else could happen to reinforce your theme. Be open to insights that come as you write. Even those of us who plot our novels sometimes benefit from the introduction of an unexpected subplot.

While writing *WayFarer,* the second novel in my Tales of Faer-aven epic fantasy series, the story took a turn into the Vale of Shadows, a place I hadn't know existed. Its inclusion in the novel was exactly right. I'm so glad I allowed the novel's hero to take me there.

One of the best ways to add subplots to the main story line is to introduce new scenes from the point of view of the characters involved in them. This is a great way to introduce secondary characters, by the way. Remember never to change viewpoints within a scene. Provide either a scene or chapter break whenever you change the point of view. Using other characters' viewpoints to tell subplots means you can introduce information to which your main character is not privy. Just remember as you weave your story lines to connect them at the end of the book. Don't leave threads hanging.

This post was first published at Janalyn Voigt's Live Write Breathe website for writers (www.livewritebreathe.com).

FORTY-ONE

Give Me a Hint: The Use of Foreshadowing

Jordyn Redwood

I was at work discussing books with a physician who is an avid reader as well of Robin Cook's novels. Cook could be considered the grandfather of the medical thriller with his groundbreaking *The Year of the Intern, which* highlighted the training physicians go through.

Cook, for me, delved into what a medical thriller should be. Take something medical in nature (like organ donation) and put a twist on it (genetically engineered individuals being used for spare body parts). That novel was *Chromosome 6*. What my physician friend said was, "The great thing about Robin Cook was he grounded you in the science before he took that leap, so when he did go over the cliff with his theory you were able to buy it hook, line, and sinker."

This conversation got me thinking a lot about my third novel, *Peril*. I'm asking the reader to take a big (HUGE really) theoretical leap, but had I spent time grounding them in how this medical theory could really play out?

That question led me to rewrite the first third of my novel.

Some people view foreshadowing as the scary thing suspense novelists do to readers to get the hair to stand up on the back of their necks. Truly, this is part of it—the scary music cuing up before the axe falls on the victim.

More importantly, though, foreshadowing could be viewed as the details we plant for readers so that when the character does something *unbelievable,* the reader won't be rolling their eyes in a jump-the-shark moment.

In my first novel, *Proof,* I needed there to be an instant in time where one character could place a lethal (or was it really?) shot to the villain. In order to do that, I had to paint a picture for the reader of the character being capable of doing it mentally and physically when that moment came.

Step One: Show that she is comfortable with weapons—and maybe a little too psychotic about her safety.

Step Two: Show that she is a good marksman. This scene included her taking a close friend to an indoor shooting gallery. Let's just say that girl had some skill even with a little bit of alcohol on board. Plus, she had purchased another weapon, which increased the probability of one of them being used. Don't give the character a weapon and then never have her use it.

Step Three: Show that she will use a weapon when in a dangerous situation. At one point in the book, the villain is giving chase and she fires at him from a moving vehicle.

Step Four: The ultimate showdown must take place. Don't plant any seeds that aren't eventually harvested.

Does anyone remember the Laura Croft *Tomb Raider* movies? In one, it dealt with her finding Pandora's Box. The whole two hours is devoted to the adventure of discovering ancient clues that would lead her to the ultimate treasure. At the end of the movie, she has the box in her hands and . . . she doesn't open it.

Huge letdown.

FORTY-TWO

Self-Editing Tips: Structure

Barbara Scott

Writing is rewriting, and rewriting is self-editing. "But isn't that the job of the editor after I've made the sale?" No. Some writers think running spell-checker is self-editing. Not so much.

"But won't rewriting my work edit the life out of it?" No, but it will catch the eye of an agent or editor as a well-written manuscript and may lead to a sale.

Obsessive editing during the writing process will destroy your work. However, after you've written the first draft, gain some distance and perspective on your manuscript by setting it aside for a few days, weeks, or a couple of months. Every writer's circumstance is unique. Now it's time to rewrite.

Think of the structure of your work as an arched bridge spanning a great river. If the contractor takes shortcuts (such as using less cement, steel, or fewer bolts) because she's bored with the process and rushes to the end, the bridge is weakened and will collapse. The same holds true for both ends of the bridge. If too much cement is used at either end of the bridge, it will collapse from the added weight.

For the purposes of this post, I'll concentrate on the structure of novels. If the structure of your story is solid, the reader will continue to turn the pages until the ending scene.

The material of the structure is comprised of the elements of the story arc (the basic story thread) held in place by a beginning, middle, and end. Pretty simplistic, huh? Yet the three-act structure has worked since Aristotle's days whether you write plays, scripts, short stories, or novels.

Some authors maintain they have a four-, five-, six-, or even eight-act structure. I maintain if you break down the parts of their story arcs, you will discover classic Aristotelian structure.

Using the bridge analogy, a car drives onto the bridge. This is the point in the novel when you can lose a reader in the first page or two. I've thrown many a book (or manuscript) on the pile beside my bed if nothing happens right away. The author might as well have written "blah, blah, blah-blah, blah."

A novel that piques the reader's interest starts as far into the story as possible. I don't want to know that the protagonist's parents left him stranded in a snowstorm when he was a toddler and that's why he's terrified of snow (or abandonment). That's backstory. The story should begin with stasis (a state of equilibrium) and then the main character, pressed with conflict, reveals her goal.

One of my favorite movies is *Indiana Jones and The Raiders of the Lost Ark*. The story throws you into the action, and then the backstory—Indy's character, profession, the setting, and the antagonist—are revealed as Act 1 plays out.

As the story progresses into the middle (Act 2) and the bulk of the novel, you should have rising and falling tension as your protagonist encounters numerous obstacles or crises.

The main turning point, or big surprise, comes in the middle of the novel. By this time the reader believes he has the story figured out. You need to turn his assumptions on their head.

The major turning point should be such a shock that no one sees it coming. It should keep your reader up at night turning pages.

The crises continue. Will he? Won't she? Oh, no! What will happen to this character your reader has invested her time in? Will everything turn out all right? How will the story ever end on a happy, satisfying note now?

Tension mounts and we reach another major turning point before we head into the final third act. Every turning point should be a surprise to the reader.

The crises are unrelenting until we reach the climax halfway through the third act. The protagonist faces off against the antagonist. The clash of the titans ensues. A woman faces her attacker or her paralyzing fear. The antagonist is not always a person. A man pushes his wife out of the path of a stampeding herd of cattle. Will he live? You get the picture.

Tie up all the loose ends of your storyline in the denouement—the final resolution of the plot or story arc. Is your ending satisfying? Does the main character live happily ever after? If you live and write in America, trust me, she better if you want to succeed as a professional author. Americans are eternal optimists.

FORTY-THREE

Twelve Qualities of a Big Story

Rachel Phifer

I love big books. I'm not talking about page count here, but stories that are so big in scope that the novels live on with me long after I finish reading. I'm even drawn to reread the story.

That's the kind of book I want to write, so before I begin writing, I analyze the bones of my story to see if it has some of those big-book qualities.

Twelve Big Book Qualities

1. <u>A Hero or Heroes</u>: Characters who take big risks and stand up for what's right. They may be deeply flawed, and yet, they're saints, magnetic leaders, or they show massive courage of some kind. They're true to life and still larger than life.

2. <u>An Impossibly Large Role to Fill</u>: Characters step into a role that at first seems much too large for them. It may be leading a dangerous military mission, stopping a plague from spreading, or rescuing one child who is falling through an emotional black hole. In the beginning, the characters aren't equipped, but as the story progresses, they learn to fill that big role.

3. <u>Injustice</u>: It can be a large scale injustice (the Nazis) or small scale (a tyrannical parent), but at all costs, it must have

high stakes and the barriers to justice must seem huge to the characters.

4. Complex Relationships: The story provides relationships that are full of great love and yet are greatly troubled. If there are complex relationships that intersect other complex relationships, that's even better.

5. A Larger than Life Setting: The setting should carry the reader away—a family vineyard, an estate house perched on a craggy coastline, a frenzied metropolis, a bustling medieval village, or a dangerous forest. If your story calls for an ordinary town or city, make sure to find its personality and drama.

6. Time Scope: There are big books that take place in a year, even in days. But there's something dramatic about watching lives take shape over a lifetime. Even a small story within the story or significant backstory can make the story feel larger.

7. Sacrifices and Crushed Dreams: A character may voluntarily give up something precious for the sake of loved ones, or their dreams may be grasped from their clenched fists. The story is bigger as they struggle to redeem the loss.

8. A Goal with Long Odds: The character—actually all of the characters—need specific goals, and they should be hard to achieve, with plenty of obstacles in the way.

9. Characters with Special Talents or Gifts: Readers love to watch gifted people work—artists, geniuses, prophets, clever detectives, explorers, brilliant doctors, even farmers if they have a special way with the land. If a character has a special calling, all the better. Starting off with only rudimentary knowledge or none, and bringing the reader along as the character learns is compelling too.

10. Souls that Don't Belong: Whether it's because of a special gift, an unusual heritage, a greater determination, their life has

set them apart somehow, and they find themselves alone in their community. Of course as the story continues, they'll find a mentor, a lover or friend, but there will be some bumpy roads before they understand that they fit together.

11. A Long Mystery or Unusual Twist: Nothing keeps readers turning the page like dropped clues along the pages as they try to solve the mystery. Also great is a dramatic mystery, which the reader understands perfectly but the characters don't. Waiting for everything to be made clear makes for great tension. Of course, any mystery or twist in a big book should have lots of personality and be critical to the character's inner life.

12. Resonating Voice: I put this last, but really it's a first. An original voice that carries the reader into the sensory and emotional experience of the novel will lure the reader in at page one and hold them until the last sentence. Voice, more than any other quality, brings me back for a second read.

FORTY-FOUR

Four Ways to Engage Fiction Readers

Dianne Christner

From listening to my readers and following book reviews, four key topics repeatedly surface. While they're not new ideas, they contain basic value in creating fictional worlds.

Readers wish to be swept away from their normal reality.

If readers wish to be swept away from their normal reality, our fiction has to contain something compelling or unique. This element must be intentional, not just something we hope for in our writing. And it should be identifiable. It can be an unusual setting or a fresh plot idea. Or how about an uplifting theme or a unique friendship? In order to offer something fresh yet appealing, I find it helpful to identify my readers and understand my genre.

Not only that, once we've swept readers off their feet, we must protect their experience by keeping them airborne—in their fictional world. They trust us not to let them come crashing back to earth without warning. Good writing remains invisible while creating a safety-net of lasting and vivid impressions. In other words, we must be careful not to do anything to draw them out of the story and ruin their fictional experience.

Readers need their emotions engaged and gratified.

126

In order to engage and gratify readers' emotions, we must create fascinating characters with whom they can identify—because they are looking for an emotional connection with the story. Our stories, and especially our endings, must not leave them up in the air, but provide emotional satisfaction and resolution. Again, we target the emotions associated with our genre. Suspense readers are looking for the adrenalin rush. They enjoy a short fall as long as they land safely in the end. Romance readers need to set their feet back on earth with a contented sigh.

Readers expect a takeaway.

Readers also expect a story takeaway. When they have to come back to reality, they want something to take with them to enrich their everyday lives. It can be a spiritual theme that gives them hope in the real world. For a mystery, it might be an unexpected and intriguing twist. In women's fiction, it might be a distinct image that provokes further thought or action—such as a family that solves their problems around the dinner table. While we foremost entertain, it's this lingering *takeaway* that lives on inside our readers' minds and excites them to spread the word about our stories. It compels them to follow our works.

Readers want to know more about authors.

Readers want to connect with us. It's humbly amazing, and it's the source of our greatest blessings. There's something very intimate in the breath of story, the giving and taking that goes into the entire fictional experience. As authors, we're sensitive beings who delight in the wonder and fear of it. And so we gladly leave our *signature*—a link for readers to interact with us or find out more about our writing.

FORTY-FIVE

Six Keys to Writing a Story with Spiritual Content

Rachel Phifer

1 . **Hook the reader.** Every good story needs a hook, including the spiritual story. Set up the spiritual story with an intriguing question and a clear goal. In *The Sparrow,* by Mary Doria Russell, we are first introduced to Father Emilio as a man who narrowly missed sainthood. He now lies in a hospital bed, sullen, uncommunicative and suspected of a terrible crime. The reader is left wondering how a godly man came to be in such a place and what his future holds now.

2. Lay the foundation for the spiritual resolution. Miracles and sudden moments of salvation may happen in real life, but will feel contrived in fiction. Not only that, but they can also be hurtful to those with unanswered prayers or who have had to work through long, hard years of healing. Build the steps toward a satisfying spiritual conclusion into the structure of the novel at every turn. The story has to earn its ending, so that when it comes, the reader will feel as if it couldn't have worked out any other way.

3. Dig for deeper themes. As important as it is to show characters accepting the gospel or to ask where God is when it hurts, those themes are common. Most likely, your novel is preaching largely to the choir, so you need to find themes that speak to the deeper struggles and goals Christians are working on as well. What does it mean to live in the light of eternity? How does prayer shape us? How do you love your enemy? How do you love your neighbor as yourself? What does a character look like who has lived out the gospel daily? And so on. When you get those rare non-Christian readers, those themes might just speak more deeply to them about the gospel than the message they've likely heard before.

4. Be fair and truthful. I once heard a theologian say that we needed to compare the best of Christianity with the best of other religions, and if you're going to look at the worst of, say, Islam or atheism, you need to be willing to look at the worst of Christianity. In the movie *God's Not Dead*, when the atheist professor breaks down and admits that he's a bitter atheist because God let his mother die, it didn't ring true. The fact is, there are many atheists who have arrived at their worldview based on careful thought, however misguided we may believe them to be. They may also happen to make decent citizens and neighbors. And we've all found our share of gossips and control freaks in church. Don't be afraid to mix it up. If you dig deeply, the light of Christ will show through all the more clearly because you've been honest.

5. Show the Sacrifice. From *A Tale of Two Cities* to *Titanic*, audiences have always stuck by a story that involves a heartfelt sacrifice. But it's the core of a Christian story. Whether it's an act of utter courage such as Hadassah going willingly to the Roman arena in *Voice in the Wind* or something more ordinary like Will laying down his pride to admit the ways he wronged his Amish relatives in *Levi's Will*, it's the sacrifice that makes the story work.

6. Show the Beauty. Sometimes writers take for granted that the resolution is what the readers want. Don't forget to show them *why* they want it. Davis Bunn shows how a prayer that has been prayed for over two thousand years comes alive when his modern character prays it in *Book of Dreams*, as if the leaves overhead were chanting the prayer with the character. Stephen Lawhead describes an old saint lit from the inside out with God's love in *Merlin*. These little moments that show the beauty of God's ways clarify the spiritual goal all the way through the book.

FAITH
HAPPENINGS.com

Are you a writer or speaker looking to grow your platform, reach and readership?

FaithHappenings.com can help you do just that!

FaithHappenings.com is an online Christian resource with 454 local websites serving more than 31,000 cities and towns. It offers tailored, faith-enriching content for members. Along with a few dozen other benefits, it connects people of faith to information about books, blogs, speaking events, and other resources that interest them most. As a writer or speaker, it will help you connect with people specifically interested in your genre, subject or brand! So, just what can FaithHappenings.com offer you?

On FaithHappenings.com You Can…

1. For Free… **List yourself as a speaker both locally and regionally**—increasing your visibility in multiple markets

2. For Free… **Announce your book signings** in your area

3. **List your books—both traditionally and self-published** (sent out to members who have requested to hear about new books in your genre)*

4. **Announce special e-book promotions the day they happen** (sent out to members and listed on the site daily!)*

5. **Build your blog traffic** by posting your blog into two categories, and be highlighted as a "Featured Blogger" on our Home Page*

6. **Be a highlighted "Author Interview."** FH Daily runs author interviews several times a week. Just email fhdaily@faithhappenings.com to see if you qualify.

7. **Create more awareness for your book with advertising!** An ad on the site is affordable for any author.*

8. As a free member yourself, you can **receive e-mail announcements for any book** in more than 70 genres

What are you waiting for? Get started today by signing up in your local area to become a member at www.faithhappenings.com.
A small fee applies

IV.

Setting the Scene

FORTY-SIX

The Anatomy of a Scene

Jan Drexler

Learning to craft good scenes for your novel is a foundational tool in your writing tool kit. Think of the scenes as the building blocks you use to construct your masterpiece. If they're faulty or incomplete, what will the building look like?

But there are as many blog posts about writing a scene for your novel as there are varieties of ice cream sundaes at your favorite summer hang out.

So why am I writing one more?

Because when it comes right down to it, writing a scene isn't as hard as it seems. You only need to break it down into four major parts:

Beginning: When the scene begins, does the reader know when and where this is taking place, and whose point of view it's in? If not, you're in danger of leaving your reader stranded in the land of floating heads. YOU may know exactly what your characters are seeing, feeling, etc., but does your reader?

Middle: The midsection of the scene should take up the most time. A sentence or two into the scene, after you've given your reader the information they need, start increasing the tension and continue to the turning point.

The turning point is the main purpose for the scene. It's where the reader learns something new about the character, or the character learns something new about himself or someone else, or a decision is made.

There are a lot of different ways this can be played out, but the main thing is to make sure the scene contributes to the flow of the story and moves things forward.

End: Does the scene resolve itself? The character(s) involved should make a decision or take an action as a result of the turning point.

And finally: Is there a hook at the end of the scene that will make the reader continue on to the next scene? Without a hook leading your reader further into the story, there is no reason for them to turn the page.

And here's a homework assignment: Look at a scene in your favorite book. Does it have all four of these elements in it? What exceptions did the author make, if any? Now do the same with one of your own scenes.

What did you learn?

FORTY-SEVEN

Seven Steps to Writing a Story in Scenes

Janalyn Voigt

You'll notice I didn't include the word "easy" in the title of this post. There are not seven "easy" steps to writing a story in scenes. It takes hard work. I suspect that's why so many writers substitute narrative summary for scenes.

Of course, when you're not sure of the components that make up a scene, it's harder to write one. If your writing seems flat or passive and you don't know why, you may have omitted one or more of the following:

Real Time: Even if you're writing in third person using past-tense verbs, lay out actions in sequential order. As a rule, especially in the beginning of your novel, don't jump backward or forward in the story. If you do, you'll interrupt the flow of time and disconcert your reader.

Characters: This element may seem like a "no-brainer." (Of course a scene will have characters.) But hear me out. Let's say you're writing about a lynch mob ready to hang an outlaw. You could state the bald fact, or you could pick faces from the crowd. Maybe the outlaw killed Jack's brother, robbed Otis's store, and held a gun to Chet's face just for fun. Having these fellows, even as minor characters, call out their grievances makes the incident personal and, therefore, more immediate.

Showing: You experience the world through your senses. Similarly, for readers to enter your written world, you must draw them through their senses. Labeling emotions is telling. It's also lazy writing. Instead of stating that Mary is sad, show her reasons for sadness, and then have her react physically and perhaps with introspection. Just don't do this in a clichéd manner. Maybe she doesn't weep but instead grows quiet or withdraws. David is angry but rather than punch a hole in the wall he exterminates every weed in his yard.

Setting: New writers often neglect this element needed to ground every scene in place and time. Using too much or not enough description is a common mistake. With too few setting details the reader will feel curiously weightless, like an astronaut floating in a zero-gravity chamber. Characters will seem like "talking heads" lost somewhere in space. If you overload your readers with description, you'll weigh them down so badly they'll barely make progress through the scene. Finding a happy balance takes practice. It helps to have feedback from great critique partners.

Action: Something physical happens, with or without dialogue. Some writers call actions that accompany dialogue "beats." Using beats instead of tags to identify speakers helps you bring a scene to life.

Dialogue: Too many writers neglect dialogue, which is a shame. It's a vital tool for characterization and for imparting information (provided you don't try to shoehorn it into your reader). You can even use dialogue to give glimpses of back story in a realistic way that doesn't disrupt your story's flow.

Purpose: Every scene must further your plot. If a scene exists merely to dump information on the unsuspecting reader, it has no real purpose and will seem aimless. Cut all such scenes and work only the information your reader needs to know into the story when your reader needs to know it.

Telling a cohesive story through scenes is an art that, once mastered, will breathe life into your writing.

FORTY-EIGHT

Four P's in a Pod

Michelle Griep

E ver try to stab a pile of peas with a fork? Inevitably, a few green roly-polys fly off your plate and plummet to the floor. It's a horrible way for a pea to go.

And even worse when it happens to one of your scenes.

Track with me here. You're writing along la-de-dah-de-dah and wham! An invisible pitchfork skewers your brain, and the words go flying right out of your head. You have no idea what to write next. And the longer you sit there, the more you wonder if the words you've already written even have a point.

Don't panic. Be proactive. Mind your P's and ... umm ... P's! Four of them to be exact: *POV, Plan, Purpose, Page Turner.* Try the following handy-dandy trick at the beginning of each scene to keep your writing on track.

POV (Point of View): This is the easiest P of all. Simply jot down from which character's perspective your reader will experience the scene.

Plan: An architect needs a blueprint to construct a building that's stable and functional. A writer needs one, too. This step is exactly what the label implies. Plan out the sequence of action for the scene, including setting and who's involved.

Purpose: If your scene doesn't have a purpose other than back story or description, then toss it out. A well-told story is one that takes the reader by the hand and pulls them along, always moving forward.

Page Turner: a.k.a. Cliff Hanger. This doesn't have to be a literal hero dangling by his hangnails from a ledge. Simply put, the goal of every scene, especially the last few sentences, is to leave the reader begging for more. Physical action is the most tangible way to accomplish this, but it doesn't have to be. Emotional or spiritual conflicts are great ways to make a reader wonder what will happen as well.

Pulling It Together: At the beginning of each scene, simply satisfy each of these "P's" before starting to write fresh copy. Here's an example of how all this pulls together (taken from my current WIP):

POV: Nicholas Brentwood

Plan: Ballroom scene / Nicholas allows Emily to dance with Henley, though he doesn't like it one bit / Shadwell asks Emily's friend Bella to dance, but Bella says she's already dancing with Nicholas / Nicholas is about to protest when he realizes not only will he be doing Bella a favor by saving her from dancing with Shadwell, but he'll have a much better view of Emily on the dance floor himself / While out dancing, he loses sight of Emily and rushes out to look for her / He searches upstairs, downstairs, everywhere, but merely turns up Emily's scare-rific 'friend' Millie, the one who's been trying to snag him / he tries to evade her, until her parting words make him stop and turn around

Purpose: Hypes up Nicholas's concern for Emily / Provides an opportunity for the next clue as to what happened to Mr. Payne

Page Turner: Millie's parting words, "I know what happened to Mr. Payne."

There you have it. It's really that simple. By thinking through the four "P's" ahead of time, words will roll right off your fingertips and appear on your screen, which technically crams one more P in the ol' writing pod . . .

Productivity.

FORTY-NINE

Making It Real

Jan Dunlap

When I first started writing my Birder Murder Mystery series, I wanted readers to feel like they were actually walking in the footsteps of my protagonist, so it was a logical choice for me to use real locations for book settings. What I didn't realize at the time was how much readers enjoy books that take place in areas they know and how much those real places can shape what I write. Once I figured out that my real locations were one of the more powerful means of attracting readers, I began using real places as much as possible, not only for marketing later, but to provide me with inspiration for other pieces of my story.

As a result, I now take detailed notes of places I visit in the course of my book research. For instance, last January, I was researching McAllen, Texas, for my next murder mystery. Since friends had recommended I try the barbeque at Fat Daddy's, I made sure I had lunch there one day. As I ate, I observed that large groups of National Guardsmen sat at many of the tables, which I also noted in my daily travel journal, along with descriptions of the patriotic posters and flags adorning the walls. When I developed my plot, I found that the soldiers I'd seen could play into my story in a critical juncture, so I wrote them in—something I never would have come up with if I hadn't personally visited Fat Daddy's. Now, when anyone from the area reads the book, they'll immediately be able to say, "This author really was here!" and it gives me the instant credibility which every fiction writer craves to lure readers into the story.

Another big benefit of writing real places into your books is that some readers identify so much with a favorite place, they tend to talk about your book simply because of the setting. In one of my books, I used a small diner where one of my daughters waitressed years ago. Not only did it give the story a strong local connection, but once it was published, the diner owners prominently displayed the book, which delighted all their customers, who then told their friends that their favorite diner was in a book. By using the diner as a piece of my story, I also didn't have to think twice about what that setting would look like, because all I had to do was describe what I saw.

Perhaps the best guideline I can provide about using real places in your fiction is the rule my publisher gave me: if you say nice things about a place, use the real name; if you want to be negative, make up a place. That should give you more readers and happier business owners (who will become your friends if they aren't already!), and much less chance of getting sued.

Who knows? You might even get a sandwich named after you . . .

FIFTY

You've Been "Notebooked"

Kariss Lynch

Have you ever read or watched a scene that gave you chills? The guy says all the right things, the girl responds accordingly, and the scene ends in an epic kiss that you feel down to your toes because you know that these two are meant for each other.

Those are the kind of scenes I like to write. And I'm still learning. Several years ago, I would have laughed at anyone who told me I would write romance. Don't get me wrong . . . I'm definitely a romantic, but I'm more of a closet romantic who only expresses it if the situation allows. As I write, I'm learning to tap into that closet romantic side of myself. To do so, it helps to understand why people love the romantic pop culture hits.

Let's face it: You can't talk pop culture romance without talking *The Notebook*.

People mock it. Chicks dig it. He's hot, and she's girl-next-door gorgeous. Guys groan when their girlfriends "Notebook" them. But there's a reason that *The Notebook* and other movies based on Nicholas Sparks' books do so well. If you can move past your bias, you'll identify the attracting factor.

It's all about love. Those are the moments in the movie/book most remembered and most quoted. Think about it. You remember what Noah said to Ally. You remember the passion and tears. You remember the words, the heartache, and the victory.

144

You root for this couple. So what can we take away that will help us write memorable romance?

1. The scene becomes another character and sets the mood.

Whether it's the sweeping southern scenes that make you long for small towns, front porches, and handsome gentlemen, or the throes of war that make you cheer for the soldiers on the battlefield, Sparks (and others) knows how to give the scene a personality all its own. The scene definitely sets the stage of the romance, tugging at your sympathies.

2. The characters are three-dimensional.

I love following Noah's story in *The Notebook*. And no, it's not just because he's good looking. I love watching his growth. He starts out as a gutsy teenager who works to help his family and experiences summer love. Only he doesn't let go when the summer comes to a close. He writes, growing in the midst of recording his heart to a girl who left. Then he heads off to war with his best friend, loses him, comes home, buys a home, loses his dad, and spends some time refurbishing a house. He is no longer the gutsy teenager out to charm the girl. He's experienced heartache, loss, success, regret, and loneliness. But then Ally comes back. He's the same romantic guy, but more mature, calm, confident in what he wants. By the end of the movie, he is an old man still set on charming his one and only love and fully confident in their love story. Who doesn't like to watch love conquer all?

3. The dialogue is memorable and passionate.

Once again, I love Noah's dialogue. This country boy is deep. Why? He realizes the cost of love, the difficulty, the pain, the joy, and he's willing and ready to weather it all. He believes it's worth it. And he makes us believe it, too.

4. Good, bad, or indifferent – it doesn't shy away from cultural issues or trends.

We live in a culture of sex, drugs, and whatever you want goes. Don't shy away from the issues. Be in the world but not of it with your writing. Some writers define love by physical relationships. We have to address how Jesus defines life and love in the midst of our romance.

5. It relates to our desire to be known, loved, and belong to something greater than ourselves.

Why is this a big deal? Because God created us for relationships, set eternity in our hearts, and said it isn't good for us to be alone. Tap into your emotions. Let them flow on the page with every word. And in the midst of the character romance, point people to the romance they can have with Jesus.

Are You In the Mood?

Jan Drexler

When you're writing a book, you have a purpose. You want to speak to your readers' emotions, bring them into your story world, and show them ideas that may change their lives.

There are many ways to do that, and one is to be purposeful in expressing the mood of your story.

The mood is different from your setting, theme, plot, or other elements of a story. The mood is the overall feeling your reader gets from your story. It can be happy, tragic, hopeful, desperate, fearful, serene . . . and everything in between. Your book will have a general mood that permeates your entire story, but each scene may have its own mood, also.

How does a writer convey mood?

There are a couple of very good ways.

First is your choice of words. Consider this excerpt from my book *The Prodigal Son Returns*:

From the simple white house nestled behind a riotous hedge of lilacs to the looming white barn, the Stoltzfus farm was the image of his Grossdatti's home, a place he thought he had forgotten since the old man's death when he was a young boy. A whisper of memory rattled the long-closed door in his mind, willing it to open, but Bram waved it off. Memories were deceptive, even ones more than twenty years old.

147

They covered the truth, and this truth was that he had a job to do. Grossdatti and his young grandson remained behind their door.

I tried to convey the feeling of nostalgia in this paragraph, so I chose soft words like "nestled," "farm," "home," "whisper," and "memory." As the paragraph reached its end, I wanted Bram to shake himself back to reality—at least his version of it. So I used harsher words like "rattled" and "truth."

Read your paragraphs aloud, listening to how the words sound. What feeling do they convey? It isn't only the meaning of words that speak to your readers – the sound does, too.

A second way to convey mood is in the construction of your sentences. Longer sentences set a softer, quieter tone, and shorter, choppy sentences convey a sense of urgency or danger.

Here's an excerpt where I was trying to show a peaceful summer afternoon:

Once the family buggy was gone, the farm settled into a quiet that Ellie seldom heard. The early summer sun was hot, and the cows had all sought the shade of the pasture. One pig's grunting echoed through the empty barn, keeping rhythm with the thump and clatter as he rubbed against the wooden planks of the sty.

Ellie wandered to the lilac bushes that surrounded the front porch of the big house, and she buried her face in the blossoms. They were nearly spent, but the scent still lingered. On either side of the front walk Mam's peony bushes held round pink and green buds. Another day or two, and they would burst into bloom.

The sentences in these paragraphs are complex, with dependent and independent clauses. They are designed to slow down the reader's pace and feel the mood of Ellie's afternoon—hot, languorous, and even lazy.

Contrast that with this excerpt:

Kavanaugh's lip curled in the sneer that was his trademark. "No cop is going to take me."

The snub nose of Kavanaugh's gun steadied as the gangster's finger tightened on the trigger. Bram shot at the same time. His body jerked as Kavanaugh's bullet hit his chest, and he fell into blackness.

The sentences here are shorter, choppier. Shorter sentences speed up the action and heighten the tension. The mood becomes urgent, dangerous and suspenseful. Interspersing longer sentences with shorter ones can draw out the tension even further.

So, have you thought about the mood of your book? It can be as elusive to pinpoint as your voice, but once you identify it, using these techniques can help you enhance it and will increase the depth of your readers' experience.

FIFTY-TWO

The World of Our Story

Henry McLaughlin

In his book *The Writer's Journey* (third edition), Christopher Vogler writes, "The Ordinary World in one sense is the place you came from last. In life we pass through a succession of Special Worlds which slowly become ordinary as we get used to them."

As writers, we often talk about creating story worlds. In reality, we create two. There is our hero's ordinary story world, the world she lives in before the inciting incident launches her into her story. Once launched, she enters the Special World of the story we are writing.

Interestingly, in many novels, the worlds may be exactly the same in terms of geography, time, economics, politics, and a myriad of other details. The world moves from Ordinary to Special when our hero decides to embark on the journey to solve the story problem or answer the story question.

Then, even if she continues to live in the same house, work the same job, go to the same church, her world becomes Special. She is now on an adventure to resolve the story problem. And that story problem transforms her world from Ordinary to Special, whether it's solving a murder, dealing with an unwanted pregnancy, or losing her spouse.

Think of the world of our lives. Everything is going along fine and then something happens. We lose a job or we get a promotion to a more challenging position, a loved one dies or a prodigal returns home, a car accident, a medical problem, a windfall. We win the lottery or we spend all our pay on lottery tickets and miss by one number.

Whatever it is, our Ordinary world becomes Special while we live through the changes until the Special World becomes Ordinary once again.

V.

Style, Language, and Voice

FIFTY-THREE

Thirteen "Tells" of a Novice Writer

Becky Johnson

In the poker-playing world, professional card sharks have a term for a novice player who inadvertently gives away the cards he's holding through some sort of gesture or tick of which he is unaware. The pros call it a "tell."

In the publishing world, professional editors and agents look for the "tells" of a novice writer whenever they scan a manuscript. With practice, we can almost always pick out the amateur from the pro from reading just a page or two. Here's a list of **Thirteen Common "Tells" of an Amateur Writer** that may give you an inside advantage at the publishing table.

1.   **Too many clichés.** If you find yourself using a common cliché, try changing it up for humor or effect. Instead of saying, "He marches to a different drum," you might say, "She rhumbas to a different drum-ba." You want to avoid clichés, but they can also be springboards to creative alternatives.

2.   **Too much telling, not enough showing**. Use scene-setting, dialogue, metaphors and gestures to show your reader an emotion. Instead of, "She felt deep sorrow," try, "She sat down and sighed heavily, staring out the

window at nothing at all. A slow trickle of tears turned to a river as her dam of resolve gave way to reality."

3. **Too much preaching/didactic tone.** Go through any nonfiction manuscript and take out words like "must" and "should" and any other words that feel like a finger-wagging nursery teacher who is scolding the reader.

4. **Sentences don't vary in length and style.**

5. **Manuscript is too text-dense.** Just looking at the page exhausts the eye because there are too many sentences crammed into one long paragraph, followed by another just as long.

6. **Page looks boring.** There are not enough "reader treats" to keep today's reader alert. Especially in our current hyper-speed world, you want to make liberal use of anything that breaks up and adds interest to the page. Pull quotes, dialogue, lists, bullet points and stand-alone sentences here and there are some ways to keep the reader engaged.

7. **Dialogue is stiff and unnatural.** The writer has not learned the art of professionally written dialogue. One sign of a pro is that they know to use a gesture to indicate the next speaker rather than over-using "he said" or "she said." For example, rather than writing, "Joy said, 'I love that crazy squirrel,'" a pro might write, "Joy laughed as she leaned toward the screen door. 'I love that crazy squirrel.'"

8. **Main character is too unlikable or too perfect.** Readers want to root for the protagonist so be careful not to make him appear either beyond redemption or too saintly. Make them flawed, human, and lovable.

9. **Too "Christianeze."** Christians are often blind to the phrases they've grown up using in church. Try sharing old religious phrases in fresh ways. Instead of, "I've been redeemed," you might say, "I knew that God had taken the mess of my life and given me, in exchange, His love."

10. **No transitions or weak transitions.** This may be the #1 "tell" of a novice. You know what you are saying and where you are going, but your reader needs a very clear bridge from your former thought to the next or they will be confused and frustrated.

11. **Old-fashioned style.** We see this in some classically trained, older writers who have not stayed current on how to grab the attention of today's internet-savvy, fast-paced reader. Read popular blogs and note the style of writing that is reaching today's generation of readers.

12. **Doesn't use the art of "hooking the reader."** You don't have long to grab the reader's attention, so you want your first two sentences to be irresistibly compelling.

13. **Doesn't end well.** Pay attention to writers who end chapters or articles especially well. There is an art to tying up a chapter or a book. In fiction and nonfiction books alike, write a sentence at the end of the chapter that propels the reader forward, making it hard for them to put your book down. I often refer to the first paragraph when summarizing an article. (See example below where I will refer back to the "poker analogy" that started this post.)

By avoiding these common novice "tells" you will soon come across as a seasoned pro, and your chances in the game of publishing will improve considerably.

FIFTY-FOUR

Balancing Clarity and Detail in Writing

Christina M. H. Powell

You want your readers to enter into the world of your book and experience in their imagination the places and events you describe as if they were there themselves in the midst of the action. Yet if your writing becomes ornate, your readers may get lost in the details and miss the point of the passage. Even worse, they may skim over the descriptive sentences, seeking the next main point. Why write words that will go unread?

Capture the Essentials

To maintain the readability of your writing while also creating vivid descriptions of people, places, and events, capture the essentials and make every word count. Choose verbs packed with meaning instead of tacking on adverbs. When describing a place, consider what senses are important to setting the scene for the passage. Is the sound of classical music playing softly in the background more essential than the color of the paint on the ballroom walls? If you are trying to set the mood for dialogue that follows, use just enough details to accomplish your goal. Create a sketch and let the reader's imagination paint in the rest of the picture.

As a reader, I find myself jumping over passages where too many clauses and adjectives abound. As a writer, I have had to remind myself that my readers will do the same.

Edit the Extraneous

After you have written a descriptive passage, edit for clarity. Cross out your favorite phrase if it detracts from the paragraph. Provide sufficient description of the attributes of an object for the reader to understand its significance. You do not need to include all the colors of the sky that make for your perfect sunset. Let the most important two or three colors set the stage.

In dialogue, the word "said" may be better than "shouted," "whispered," or "intoned." While those other words convey a richer meaning, they may break up the continuity of the conversation. Let the words of the speakers carry the content. Remove nonessential dialogue that does not carry the plot or illustration forward. Jump into the action without providing too many trivial details. In short, get to the point and remove material that will confuse the reader.

Check for Flow

Your paragraphs of writing describing a majestic waterfall at the edge of the forest may be poetic and beautiful, but if they interrupt the flow of the chapter, prepare to edit. While writing my first book, *Questioning Your Doubts: A Harvard PhD Explores Challenges to Faith*, I wrote illustrations to enhance the point I was making. I learned from reader feedback that the illustrations worked best when they were entertaining but concise. If I spent too many sentences telling a story, the reader's train of thought might be broken, defeating the purpose of the illustration.

On the other hand, writing that sparkles with clarity can seem too clinical without enough descriptive material. Coming from a scientific background, I am used to conveying challenging topics in clear and precise sentences. When I first started writing my book, I had to give myself permission to tap into my creative writing side and add poetic elements to my prose. Too much clarity can lead to short, choppy sentences that need more descriptive elements to weave them together into the tapestry of the chapter.

FIFTY-FIVE

Hearing What You Can't Read

Jennie K. Atkins

I am always fascinated by our five senses—touch, smell, sight, taste, and hearing. I love the warmth of my husband's hand when he clasps mine, the fragrant scent of a rose caught up on the morning breeze, or the tart pucker of a Granny Smith apple.

As writers, we know that adding the senses into our books makes the world our characters live in more real to the reader. But that's not where I'm going with this post. My question to you is, when was the last time you listened to a book? I don't mean just for pleasure, but to get into the depth of the story by using more than your eyes.

I have a Kindle that offers a "text to speech" option, which I've found to be available on many books. (I believe this is up to the author and/or publisher if they offer this choice and I'm sure it's available on other readers as well.) It has a computer generated voice, which for me is fine, but you can go through this exercise with an audio book as well.

The trick is to listen to the words, but not become caught up in the story. It's amazing what you can hear.

Rhythm: Did you know words and sentences have rhythm? When you listen to a story you can hear it. A good writer will create a steady beat with their words to slow the pace of the story. Or, they may speed it up to raise the tension as needed.

Choice of words: I'm a big proponent of not using the same word over and over again. I'm not advocating pulling out a thesaurus and running the gamut of possible choices, but just having an acute awareness of word choices. It makes the work more appealing. Fresh. You can "hear" the repeated words more than "read" them.

Story world: Has the author "painted" the world the character is in vividly enough that when you close your eyes while listening to a scene you can almost imagine yourself right in the middle? This aspect is hard to do when you need your eyes to read!

Emotions: Much like the story world, can you picture the characters' actions? Feel their pain? Or laugh with them? This follows the line of showing instead of telling. When you listen to a book, you can "see" their reaction, like a movie screen playing on the backside of your eyelids.

I go through this exercise with many of my favorite authors. I take the time to learn from their writing style by listening to it. Then try to apply the concepts to my own writing.

So what do I do then? I always listen to what I've written. I email the Word doc to Amazon and it goes right to my Kindle. Then I go through the same exercise. Have I set the proper rhythm for the scene? Do I have words repeating that should be changed? Have I created a memorable scene mixed with real-life emotions?

Try it sometime. You might be surprised what you hear that your eyes never would have seen.

FIFTY-SIX

What's Your Point of View?

Julie Cantrell

When I wrote my debut novel, *Into the Free*, I never gave much thought to point of view; but as the words began to hit the page, they naturally fell into first-person narration.

First-person narration tells the story from the point-of-view of one character in a novel (usually the protagonist), and makes use of the words "I" and "me." Critics point out that this style limits the perspective because it doesn't allow readers to access other characters in the story. While this is a viable opinion, I argue that first-person allows the reader to gain even greater perspective by viewing the universe from the lens of that one character on a much more intimate level than anything an omniscient third-person narrator can provide. (We'll leave second-person for another day.)

Yes, the view of other characters will be skewed by that one character's interpretation of their actions, appearance, etc., but readers are granted full-access into the brain of that one narrating voice, even more so when that narrator is a trustworthy character who isn't deceiving us as we read. Essentially, we, as readers, are allowed to become that character. This enables us to enter that character's world, interacting with the other characters, experiencing the events, and engaging at every sensory level throughout the story.

163

When an author delivers a story in first-person, we close the book feeling as if we have lived to tell the tale. This intrusive point of view makes the entire reading experience personal for us, moving it from the level of observation to participation. And because, by nature, the first-person perspective limits every scene to those in which the narrator is actively present (or his/her memory of such), we aren't forced to pull back and watch something happening across space or time. We have no choice but to dive right into every single event of the story. We feel it, taste it, smell it, and react to it cognitively, emotionally, and instinctually.

As a reader, I have always enjoyed reading first-person narrations. Some of my favorite books were written using this point-of-view, and as a result, the narrators have become some of my favorite characters. Consider Scout in Harper Lee's *To Kill a Mockingbird*, Holden Caulfield in J.D. Salinger's *Catcher in the Rye*, or Nick Carraway in *The Great Gatsby*, who tells us the tragic love story between Gatsby, Daisy, and Tom from his perspective.

<u>Writing prompt:</u> If you're stuck in a scene, try writing it from another character's point-of-view. What can you learn from seeing the event from a different perspective?

FIFTY-SEVEN

Hooptedoodle and You

Heather Ijames

You know the thing about writing styles, right? How they're like our beloveds' faces. Beauty in the eye of the beholder and all that other pomp and parade. The skinny guy loves the fat chick, but no one knows why, except them. And that's all that matters. The same goes for writing styles. Some styles click for readers and others repulse them.

And while styles range from aristocratic splendor to colloquialisms at the john, I've learned that the only authentic way to find out who I am as a writer was to first discover who I wasn't.

Consider the following nugget of prose:

"The sun rose like a uniformed officer in full salute, beckoning me to face the day with equal vigor."

Yes, many authors are entitled to write like this, and do a splendid job at it. I commend them. It's not me, though. I tried to make it me, but failed. I'd probably write it like this: "Ah, cripes. The sun's up. Shoot it or me. You decide."

Not to mention that if one of my characters was privy to someone regaling in the sun in the same manner as in the first scenario, they'd push said regaler to the ground and rob them of loose change to buy a pumpkin spice latte. Not looking back at the sun, no, not even once.

My style, of course, doesn't resonate with everyone, and for that, hoorah. Because if it did, then there'd be a whole lot more people doing a whole lot more shoving and robbing for pocket change. And, that's just bad business for us as a society, don't you think?

(I kid. Reserve the hate mail for when I talk politics or let my kids run wild at the mall.)

It's important to dip your toes into the styles of others. Not to emulate, per se, but to see what hits home with you and what simply slaps you ugly.

You never know, the constant searching might help you find your anthem, as I've found mine. You see, when people criticize me for having too minimalistic of a style, I can now tell them to take their hooptedoodle out for a nice steak dinner and smooch it.

That's right. Hooptedoodle. Courtesy of the one and only Steinbeck.

"Sometimes I want a book to break loose with a bunch of hooptedoodle. The guy's writing it, give him a chance to do a little hooptedoodle. Spin up some pretty words maybe, or sing a little song with language. That's nice. But I wish it was set aside so I don't have to read it. I don't want hooptedoodle to get mixed up in the story. So if the guy that's writing it wants hooptedoodle, he ought to put it right at first. Then I can skip it if I want to, or maybe go back to it after I know how the story come out."

–*Sweet Thursday* by John Steinbeck

FIFTY-EIGHT

Writing Powerful Sentences

Rachel Phifer

On my writing journey, I spent a lot of time studying the big-picture concepts of writing, such as story arcs, conflict and character, but then I began to notice some smaller-scale aspects. A phrase or a small block of text would sing out to me as I read. For a while, I logged the best examples in an Excel spreadsheet. I noticed that my favorite books usually had a lot of these winning sentences.

What made them so powerful? Just as I had studied scenes and novels to see what made them successful, I began to study phrases and individual sentences to see what gave them that singing quality. All of them had one of the six qualities below. Most had several of them.

The Five Senses
The authors didn't just use the senses. They bathed the words in sight or touch or taste (often using more than one sense at a time) until I could smell the burning gasoline or feel the dried leaves crumble between my own fingers.

"There was a sizzle and steam and a sound like a thousand muskets firing. Then the sheets of ore began to fall."
–Year of Wonders, *Geraldine Brooks*

Emotion

167

The phrases usually occurred in the context of an emotional scene, but then a few well-chosen words would zing the emotion all the way home.

"I had only human comparisons for such a look. Caesar and Brutus. Jesus and Judas."

–The Host, *Stephenie Meyer*

Metaphorical Language

The authors utilized metaphors or similes, fresh images that made general ideas tangible and ordinary actions captivating.

"The prayer seemed to find shelter in the morning breeze, as though chanted by the leaves overhead."

–Book of Dreams, *Davis Bunn*

Rhythm

Repetition of a word or a sentence structure gave the writing rhythm, almost like poetry.

"Each question would lead to another and another until there was only a man and a woman in a garden and a forbidden tree."

–At the Scent of Water, *Linda Nichols*

Forceful, Visceral Words

Even removed from their scenes and sentences, the words were strong, capable of evoking a reaction. I noticed that the writers often used words related to the body (bone, blood, flesh) or to a threat (thunder, electric, knifed). Even when the words were used in a different context (neither related to a human body or a physical threat), they still carried the weight of those associations.

"Her voice was a whip-crack in the silent arena."

–Taliesin, *Stephen Lawhead*

Unique

The text twisted the normal way of saying things. The writers clearly dug deep, looking for an original and unexpected way to convey their scene, and the words they found were guaranteed to catch the reader's attention.

"She had skin the shade of bootleg coffee, and crossing her back were the memories of lashed scars."

–Harvesting the Heart, *Jodi Piccoult*

Once I pinned down what gave these memorable sentences their power, it was that much easier to write a few of my own.

FIFTY-NINE

Showing Versus Telling

Jordyn Redwood

Let me first say I am hardly an expert on show versus tell— every writing teacher's admonition for every storyteller out there. In fact, I was quite shocked when another author said she was taking notes on some passages in *Poison* because she thought they were good examples of showing. I am still hoping she will tell me exactly which ones they were so I can admire my own amazing work because I was *that* surprised.

Showing versus telling can definitely be learned (after all, I did it and was never an English major) so don't go over the writer's cliff Thelma and Louise style if some of these points don't hit home. I am still learning the more advanced points myself and that's a mark of a true writer—always desiring to learn more.

The concept of showing could also be described as Deep POV. I think these concepts are honestly interchangeable. So if you hear one—think of the other.

The first (and really good) piece of advice I got on showing was to write my scenes as if I was filming a movie. How would I describe what was on the screen to a reader without stating the obvious?

For instance: *He was angry.* This is telling. It doesn't leave any room for the reader to use their imagination. Now, more showing. *Her husband swore at her and spittle hit her face seemingly to mark a target for his fist to punch her in the jaw.* See the difference? I haven't said the word "angry" at all, but does this man seem fired up?

While editing, you're likely telling if you name the feeling. He was mad, sad, fearful . . . etc.

A great tool I've used to help me show more visceral reactions is *The Emotion Thesaurus.* There is also a website by the same author called The Bookshelf Muse. It gives specific bodily actions for tons of different emotions. Use this as a starting point to generate ideas and then improve them for your own manuscript.

Another tip to help show instead of tell is to phrase things as questions. Telling: *She wondered if her attacker was walking behind her.* Showing: *The echo of footsteps matched her high heels as they clipped down the pavement of the dark alley. Was it him? Was it the man who nearly killed her with a quick slash of a knife across her throat two years ago? The one she presumed was now sending her all those threatening letters—just like before. Now he was free.*

To show more, add a visceral reaction from the woman from the emotion she is likely feeling which in this instance would be fear.

The echo of footsteps matched the quickened pace of her heart as she broke out into a run down the dark alley. Instinctively, her hand covered the thick scar as a shield from both the memory and the act. Was it him? Was it the man who nearly killed her with a quick slash of a knife across her throat two years ago? The one she presumed was now sending her all those threatening letters—just like before. Now he was free.

I know—future editor. How can she run with her hand set on her throat? Just to illustrate a point. Edit at will.

Also, don't feel like you have to do this in the first draft. The first draft is all about getting the words on the page. Showing can be added in subsequent editing phases that you do before the manuscript goes to an agent or publisher, but don't get too hung up on trying to do a lot in the first draft until it becomes more natural for you.

This is just the beginning. There are many more techniques that can be used so keep working at it and you'll have the reader sitting inside your character in no time.

SIXTY

Are You a Story Crafter or a Storyteller?

Janalyn Voigt

In many ways, the world of book publishing parallels that of musical performance. Both are beautiful, exhilarating, and demanding. And both can sap creativity. Where the ultimate product is art, inevitable conflicts between the needs of business and creative expression exert themselves. When it comes to breaking in those with technical brilliance have an advantage, but to rise to the top, something else is needed.

I once represented my college as the soprano member of a vocal quartet in an honors choir made up of students from colleges throughout the western United States. We prepared on our own, and then met for three long days of intense rehearsal. Yes, there was glitz and glory in our single performance, but it wasn't that I remember most about the experience but something that happened during one of the rehearsals.

I don't even remember which musical passage we were struggling with at the time, but our accomplished director refused to let us get away with good enough. He pushed us, irritatingly so, until in a moment of delirious harmony, glorious sound filled the rehearsal chamber. In the awestruck silence that followed tears pricked my eyes.

Our director thumped his chest. "Ever feel *that*?" He paced before us, meeting eyes. "You all have a lot going for you, but no matter how technically brilliant you become, the ability to *feel* the music is what will help you most. Never lose that."

I have never forgotten his words. In my studies I knew students who could execute a passage of music to perfection but who lacked the passion to bring it alive. By contrast, I have seen a graying grandmother with a quavering pitch move an entire congregation to tears with her simple song. I say this not to invalidate the quest for excellence but to illustrate that feeling the music always trumps craft.

In writing, there is storytelling and story crafting. Yes, we must strive to perfect our craft and even consider our market's wishes, but it's even more important to tell a story that resonates on a deep level. If we lose our passion for story, we will also lose readers. It's not enough to hone our craft until it shines. Producing a story that sings should cost in terms of creativity, drawn as it is from our very soul. It is this that separates artists from artisans.

Because writing does not exist as art alone, however, I will add some technical tips for engaging reader's emotions. I almost hesitate to do so, in case anyone latches onto these techniques as the way through. They illuminate the story path but are not the path itself.

Tap a universal experience. A mother's arms, teenage acne, and rejection in love are but a few commonalities to which we all can relate. Writing about universal experiences in an evocative way breathes life into writing.

Write to the senses. Use taste, touch, smell, sight, and sound to bring a fictional world to life. The more vividly you imagine your story's scenes, the easier this becomes.

Show rather than tell. Create fully-realized scenes readers can step into. Narrative has its place to help in pacing as it skips us past unnecessary details, but most often passages of telling would be better if written as scenes. I got tired of hearing this advice given by rote with no explanation of *how* to do this, so I filmed the video "5 Ways to Show Not Tell in Fiction Writing" for my Live Write Breathe site for writers.

Create a sympathetic situation for your main character. The reader wants to identify with and care about the main character. Provide a gripping opening scene to meet your reader more than halfway. Be careful here, though. There's a difference between engaging a reader's emotions and manipulating them. Being faithful to your true story will guide you.

Have someone react. Not allowing room for reaction is a common failing, but this technique is so powerful it should never be ignored. As an example (spoiler alert), in the movie *The Hunger Games*, when Rue dies, the heroine grieves for her. If she didn't, we wouldn't feel the loss as deeply as we do. The riots that break out are also a reaction that stirs our anger at the injustice of the games.

Hone your craft. Nothing pulls a reader out of a story faster than clumsy storytelling, so do study craft. But remember that craft is no substitute for inspired storytelling.

There will always be tension between the business and art of writing, but that doesn't have to be bad, not when you consider that the best fiction marries fine storytelling with excellent story crafting. It is even possible to thrive in the tension between business and art.

SIXTY-ONE

Five Writing Rules I've Learned from Pixar

Dena Dyer

My family adores Pixar movies. Every year, we look forward to their latest release, impatiently marking time until we can immerse ourselves in whatever new world they've created. We're such fans of the studio that we even have their Digital Shorts collections.

As a mom of youngsters, I've spent countless hours in theaters watching duds [I'm not naming names, but I just saw a new movie from another animation studio, and it was a real turkey. BTW, whoever brought the disaster called *Gnomeo and Juliet* onto the big screen—I want those two hours of my life back. And my money, preferably with interest.]

However, I almost always enjoy Pixar flicks. The minds that dreamed up *Monsters, Inc.* and *Cars* inspire me. Because I have the privilege of teaching writing to aspiring authors, I've begun to study Pixar's methods in order to share them with my students. What have I learned?

1) **Story is king.**

The Pixar folks spend *years* perfecting the story of their movies before they ever move on to the animating process. Wow.

In my own writing journey, I've learned not to "tell" (relate things that happened so readers can understand how that situation changed me) and instead "show" (include dialogue, characters, and movement). No matter what genre you write in, good storytelling is essential. Today's art consumers are savvy, busy, and distracted. I know, because I am one. We want to be swept away by an immersive tale, not be told what we should learn from a situation.

2) Be tenacious.

Wall-E and *Finding Nemo* director Andrew Stanton admits that in the early years, Pixar employees created mostly by instinct and made a lot of mistakes. However, they wouldn't give up or give in to the pressure to do what had been done before.

They also work like fiends to get the characters and settings right. I found a few stats which blew my mind. There were:

- 3,473,271 individually animated hairs on the Lots-o-Huggin Bear from *Toy Story 3*
- 2,320,413 individually animated hairs on Sully in *Monsters, Inc.* (It took 11 to 12 hours to animate a single frame featuring Sully!)
- 1,150,000 individual hairs rendered on *Ratatouille's* hero, Remy.

Wow again.

3) Invoke wonder.

Pixar has mastered this. The writers and animators help us feel again what we often felt as children—awe, gratitude, and joy.

Here's an exercise: Think about the first time you tasted ice cream, if you can remember it. Or the first time you saw something that took your breath away. Now write about it.

Wonder is ineffable, but if we can draw on it and re-create it in a scene, we've captured our audience's attention immediately. They will follow us almost anywhere we lead them.

4) **Take risks.** A rat learning to be a chef? Preposterous. A film about a robot from the future with no dialogue for 45 minutes? Absurd. Kids' movies beginning with the death of characters? Totally insane.

But they work. They work because the guys and gals behind those stories make us forget we're watching animated films. They work because–due to great storytelling–we care about the characters, and we relate to them in some way. Which brings me to my last point.

5) **Do your homework.**

Too many films are built on flimsy premises. While the finished products might be technically sound, their foundation is cracked, and the outside shiny-ness simply can't make up for creaky scaffolding, bored talent, and cheap materials. Often, the stories are weak and the jokes seem more important than plot.

Audiences can tell when authors know what they're doing and when they don't. We don't have to write only about what we've learned from our experiences, but we have to make time for research, education, and paying our dues. Even after all his success, Stanton told an audience in 2012 that he had recently taken an acting seminar to learn more about what drives characters.

I respect that. I bet you do, too.

SIXTY-TWO

Writing with Style

Christina M. H. Powell

All writers want to write with style. However, your publisher thinks of style less in terms of crafting words with fashion and flair and more in terms of communicating with good grammar and consistency. Here are a few resources you will need as you polish your prose for publication:

1. Manual of Style: A manual of style (MOS or MoS) is a comprehensive guide to editorial style and publishing practices. These thick books cover industry-wide or profession-wide guidelines for writing. If you are writing a book for general readership, you probably need to follow *The Chicago Manual of Style*. For both UK and US usage, you can turn to the *New Oxford Style Manual*.

If you are writing articles for newspapers or magazines, you may need *The Associated Press Stylebook*. If you are writing for a scientific or medical audience, you will need to use the *AMA Manual of Style*. Other academic fields and professions have specific manuals of style. I keep several manuals of style handy on a bookshelf near my writing desk. All of these reference books provide guidelines for grammar, citing sources and use of terms specific to that writing style. They also help you better understand the publishing process and the final layout you can expect for the piece you are writing.

2. Publisher's Style Guide

The publishing house for your book may have its own style guide that serves as a supplement to an industry-wide manual of style. InterVarsity Press, the publisher of my book, *Questioning Your Doubts: A Harvard PhD Explores Challenges to Faith*, provided me with an editorial style guide that addressed how they format parts of a book and answered specific questions about grammar, punctuation, word usage and appropriate choice of abbreviations. Remember that your publisher's style guide can overrule a more general manual of style, so always follow your publisher's editorial direction.

3. Style Sheet

While writing a book or an article, you might find that certain words or phrases could be spelled, capitalized, punctuated, abbreviated or used in more than one way. To keep your writing consistent, create a style sheet that tracks your own or your editor's rules for these words and phrases. This style sheet will take precedence over the more general publisher's style guide and the industry-wide manual of style. Make a simple template with two columns: one that lists each word or rule and one that defines the style. Fill in the template as you write or receive comments from your editor.

A style sheet also can help you achieve consistency across a series of articles for the same magazine or for each book in a trilogy. It can save you time when editing your final draft by eliminating the need to look up a given rule in a larger reference work or trying to locate a particular email from your editor. With style sheets, guides and manuals helping you handle the mechanics of writing, you will have creative energy left over for the fun part of writing, such as choosing great literary devices and playing with the rhythm of a sentence. Within the constraints of proper style, your own writing voice will emerge.

VI.

Process

SIXTY-THREE

Stitching Your Story

Jan Drexler

W e were almost ready to begin our ladies' Bible study the other night when Sandi asked about my writing. I told her about the revisions I'm working on, and how they'll make my story better.

Then she leaned back in her chair, shook her head, and said, "I don't know how you do it. I don't know how you write books like you do!"

I knew I had the perfect analogy for her. Sandi is a quilter, and she'd understand: *Writing a book is like making a quilt.*

First you select a design, the "big picture" of your finished quilt.

For a book, the "big picture" is the genre and basic plot.

As you make the design of your quilt your own, you choose colors and patterns. You spend hours selecting just the right fabrics to fit your design.

As you plot your book, you develop characters with goals, motivations, and conflicts. You choose a setting that will complement the plot. And you work on your story structure, plotting or outlining the way it works best for you.

When you start constructing your quilt, you work on one block at a time, stitching each piece into place.

When you start writing your novel, you work on one scene at a time—beginning, middle and end—stitching with words rather than thread.

Finally, you lay all your quilt blocks out on the floor to see how the finished project will look—and then you revise the design by moving blocks around and creating different color combinations.

And your novel? Revisions are part of the process! Switch that scene to a different character's point of view. Rearrange the chapters to bring your antagonist into the picture earlier. Ramp up that happily-ever-after ending!

And last of all, when everything else is done, you finish your quilt by stitching the layers together and binding the edges, sealing the work you've done.

With your novel, it's the work of editing and polishing that puts the final stamp on the story.

But the thing quilting and writing have most in common? The finished product is a work of your heart that you share with others.

SIXTY-FOUR

Concrete Tips on Book Writing: It's Like Working a Puzzle

Gillian Marchenko

Just how *does* one go about writing a book?

Have you ever had that thought?

I am a published author and most days, I still struggle with that question. There's so much involved in writing a book: craft, connections, moxie, perseverance.

And then there's this, too: **writing is vulnerable.** Edna St. Vincent Millay said "a person who publishes a book willfully appears before the populace with his pants down."

But what else can we do? We must write. And sometimes our efforts turn into a book.

I am in the process of writing my second book, which has pretty much eclipsed everything else in my life. With my first book, I took years writing the whole manuscript before finding an agent and a publishing house. This time, my agent sold the book on proposal with a deadline. I was given eleven months to write and submit it. Yikes.

But how do you actually *do* **it?**

I've decided that, either way, whether you are on deadline or on your own agenda, writing a book is like doing a puzzle.

I write creative nonfiction. My puzzle pieces are anecdotes and stories from my life. I lurch around in the darkness of my writing cave, type words, peel back memories and scenes from the past, and try to find something salvageable to get down on paper. I try pieces in different places, and attempt to trust that the piece has a place, and that at some point the puzzle will be complete.

Yeah, but, can you answer the question?

Oh, right, I'm supposed to give you a few concrete tips on writing a book.

Let's assume you are a writer. Here are skills you already possess: you read a lot, you write, you have taken classes or participated in a writing workshop that critiqued your work. Let's assume you are ready to write a book, and you are looking for a few quick, concrete tips regarding the process.

OK, I can help with that.

-**I prepare.** I read a chapter from a book I love. I pray about my writing. I block common distractions (i.e. if the kids are home, it is off to the coffee shop I go). I look at my calendar on Google and plan writing time. It is as official as doctor appointments and school functions.

-**I write.** I can't tell you how many people have talked to me about writing. "How much of the story do you have down?" I ask. "Oh, I haven't started writing yet. It's all up here." (Points to head). Yeah, no, that's not going to work. I try to find several hours to write. I shoot for 1,000 words or two hours editing. I spend time looking off into space, though, too.

-**I realize that it takes a lot of work.** It took me years to write the first draft of *Sun Shine Down*. And just so you know, nobody writes wonderful first drafts (if they do, I am going to avoid them and refuse to read their work on principle). *Rewriting* is key. I hired a professional editor, printed out her suggestions, sat down to the blank page, and re-typed the whole thing.

-**I look for tools that will help.** I purchased Scrivener, a word processing program specifically for writers. I can pop in and out of chapters easily and I love the corkboard feature that helps me see the big picture of my book. I also found an app in Google Chrome based on the Pomodoro Technique. It blocks social media for 25 minutes and then gives me 5 minutes to check email or get up before returning to work. Keep your eye out for tips and tools that will help you and then go a step farther, and utilize them.

-**I try to ignore negativity.** Beware. Throughout the process you will assume you can't do it. After, God willing, your book publishes, you still won't believe you did it or that you could do it again. One of the best ways I know to ignore negativity is to keep writing. I also talk to other writers and attend a monthly writing group.

The second half of Millay's quote is "If it is a good book nothing can hurt him. If it is a bad book nothing can help him."

So, here's to good books! Here's to puzzle pieces in place, and here's to us in our writing pursuits!

SIXTY-FIVE

Everything I needed to Know About Writing I Learned from My Dad's Level

Amy K. Sorrells

When I was a little girl, Saturdays were my favorite day of the week, because Dad took me to the hardware store. Never a man without a project, Dad and I strolled the aisles and picked out all the uber-cool and necessary items. Back home, he let me watch him build.

Even as an adult, Dad builds projects around our house: corner benches, window seats, entertainment cabinets, wainscoting, and more. I've often thought about tackling carpentry projects myself, but I've always been afraid his gifts of patience, precision, and measurement didn't pass down through the genetic pipeline.

Until last week, that is. I gulped hard, then set about transforming a small, unused closet in my son's room into a book nook, complete with a seat, shelves, and trim. As I worked, I couldn't help think of how similar building and woodworking are to the craft of writing. So, here for you today are the top ten applicable things I learned:

1) Borrowing ideas from others is a compliment. I found the book nook idea at my favorite DIY blog, Thrifty Decor Chick. I

copied some of the ideas, but ultimately, the project quickly became unique to my home and my son's personality. Application: Don't be afraid to consider how to tweak popular (even Shakespearean) story lines into your own masterpiece.

2) Sketch out a plan. I drew sketches with all my ideas and at all sorts of angles. This really helped when I took it to the hardware store and explained my ideas to Mr. Friendly-But-Skeptical-of-a-Female-Builder in the blue apron. Application: Plot and outline. And know that girls can build, too.

3) Take time to measure. And measure again. I measured most boards at least three times before cutting them. Even so, I had to take some pieces back to the saw for additional trimming, because of angles I hadn't anticipated. Application: Research. And research more. You may not need all the research you gather for your story, but it's better to have too much than not enough. You can't make a piece of wood longer, after all.

4) The level never lies. My Dad always spends more time leveling than he does nailing and drilling. As a young girl, this seemed like a waste of time. Now, with one (fairly) successful project under my belt, I understand how one unlevel board can ruin the whole project. Application: You can never fact check or edit too much.

5) Shims come in handy. A side board which supported the nook's seat wasn't level. I added a shim to the low end to make it right before I drilled the seat plank on. Sitting crooked wouldn't be much fun. Application: Take time to smooth out and adjust your prose.

6) Sometimes you have to yank out a bent nail. I stink at hammering. Should be the easiest part of a project, right? Not for me. I'm hammer challenged. Inevitably, at least a few of my nails bend, and I'm tempted in frustration to just hammer them

in anyway. Sideways. Application: Don't be sloppy. Take your time.

7) When stuck, ask a master for help. Switch projects for a moment: Last winter I painted my kitchen yellow. Three times. After the first two shades came out neon and lemonish and all wrong, I bawled like a baby knowing I'd have to paint the whole room a third time. I called my Dad. We knocked it out in a couple hours. Application: Read and talk to established authors. They help get you out of writing ruts.

8) Wood putty and spackle are my new best friends. For holes. Dings. Application: Edit.

9) Sandpaper makes all the difference. Application: Edit some more.

10) Invest in a good paintbrush. The final touches of a project are when I'm most tempted to take shortcuts. I'm tired of looking at the mess. I just want to get 'er done. But alas, these are the moments which make a project shine. I found out the hard way that using a crappy paintbrush when applying high gloss paint to cabinetry looks plain awful. Application: Don't skimp before hitting the send button. Edit again.

Yes.

One.

More.

Time.

SIXTY-SIX

Using a Plot Board to Plot Your Novel

Erica Vetsch

In Part II of this book, I wrote about how a Plot-First Writer Builds Character(s). I admitted to being a plot-first writer and a dedicated 'Plotter.' Boy howdy, if you want to divide a room full of novelists quicker'n Shergar won the Derby, ask who is a plotter and who is a 'pantser.'

But, though novelists fall mostly into two camps, each side often wonders about how the other manages to write books using their method. I thought I'd give you a peek into my plotting method.

I use a plot board. I first came across this idea on the Seekerville blog (seekerville.blogspot.com) where a guest had a photograph of her own plot board. Since I'm a visual person, I glommed onto the idea and created a board of my own to see if it would work for me too.

And it sure does! There are so many things I love about using my plot board. The plot board allows me to see at a glance how many scenes I have, who is the point-of-view character, and the characters' Goals, Motivations, & Conflicts. It forces me to write out, however briefly, the internal and external goals of the characters and really think about what it is I'm trying to say with the story. Oh, and I get to play with post-it notes.

One other thing I love is that it's easy-peasy to change your mind about something. You just move the post-it to a new place or throw it away and write out a new one. I found this particularly appealing, especially since I tend to change my mind a lot while plotting.

The top half of my plot board is divided into 20 equal sections and numbered across the rows. Each of the numbered boxes represents a chapter in the story. (Twenty is just a starting point. I lengthen or shorten the story based upon what is needed. But there is only room for about 20 boxes on the plot board. If I need more, I have to scrunch things and overlap.) The bottom half is divided into two parts with six equal sections in each part. These are for the characters.

Prior to writing anything out for the plot board, I've researched, ruminated, and spent days and weeks reading and thinking about the story. I've got a few high points of the plot in my head, and I have a fair idea of setting, time period, etc. I have a rudimentary idea of the characters, too. This pre-plotting prep is necessary for me. If I dive into plotting too early, before the story has had a chance to marinate in my subconscious, I find myself staring at the blank plot board the same way I stare at a blank screen if I haven't plotted beforehand.

When it comes time to begin filling in my plot board, I start at the bottom of the board with the two six-chambered grids. On each side, one column is labeled *External,* and one is labeled *Internal.* This is where I put the Goals, Motivations, and the Conflicts for each of the two main characters. Since I write romance, this means the hero and the heroine. *What do they want, why do they want it, and what is keeping them from getting it?* I decide what personality types my characters are (click on the first link in this post to see how I do that) and start plotting the story.

Then I grab my smallest post-its, about 1.5 x 1 inch. I write the major plot points out and stick them to a notebook page. (Things like *Avalanche hits Train,* or *Finds Out He's Adopted.*) As fast as the ideas come to me, I jot them down, keeping it brief and fairly broad. When I think I've got the big ideas of the story set down, I start arranging them on the plot board. I keep them in chronological order, but I don't sweat too much whether they are in their final position or not. I know it's probably going to change as I go. When I have the bones of the story down, I start making logical connections with scenes. *What has to happen in order to get the character from major plot point one to major plot point two?* I use the next larger size post-it for these in various colors. Pink for the heroine's POV and blue for the hero's. Orange, yellow, purple, chartreuse . . . those are for secondary characters' POV scenes. By color coding the post-its, I can see at a glance if I've kept a good balance of his/her scenes and if I've lost anyone in the shuffle.

One thing I mustn't forget to mention is that the whole time I'm doing this, I'm talking. Usually to my daughter. By talking it out and letting someone not as familiar with the story ask "Why?" kinds of questions, I minimize the plot holes as much as I can up front. My daughter is great at this, and I plot much better and quicker when she's involved in the process.

When I get all the scenes filled in, I tell the story once more aloud, making sure I have it the way I want it. Then I use the plot board to type out a chapter-by-chapter, scene-by-scene synopsis, including what I want to accomplish in each scene. I know without a doubt that when I have that road map in my mind and in my hands, I write much faster than if I'm feeling my way around with no idea where I'm supposed to be going.

So there you have it. My plotting system. It works for me, and it's been tweaked and refined each time I go through the process of plotting a new story. I hope you can glean something that will help you.

SIXTY-SEVEN

Organizing Ideas into an Outline

Christina M. H. Powell

The bridge between brainstorming great ideas to fill the blank pages of your book and coherent writing that communicates your message to readers is a detailed chapter-by-chapter outline.

But how do you begin to organize all the puzzle pieces of ideas?

Write down your random ideas

Like someone preparing to solve a jigsaw puzzle, you need to gather your ideas without worrying how they fit together. Collect your thoughts on a piece of paper or type them down the page of a Word document. If you must, scribble on a napkin as creativity strikes. Decorate your desk with post-it notes. Just capture the ideas and spread them out like puzzle pieces on a table.

When writing my first book, *Questioning Your Doubts: A Harvard PhD Explores Challenges to Faith,* I thought of illustrations and concepts that helped to communicate the main concepts in a certain chapter. I knew those ideas would shape the paragraphs yet to be written, but I needed more time to figure out how to make those ideas flow together. My first step was to capture those ideas and polish them into gemstones in their own isolated and random paragraphs. The process of stringing the gemstones together to make jewelry would come later.

Look for relationships between ideas

How do you begin to work a section of a jigsaw puzzle? I usually start by grouping together the pieces with similar colors or the pieces that have complementary shapes. Like a jeweler preparing to make a bracelet out of polished gemstones, I think about patterns. Before writing an outline for a book, I consider the relationships between the ideas in the chapter. Do I need to present the ideas in a chronological order? Should I arrange concepts next to each other in a way that creates contrast between different ideas? Should I build reader interest by adding a little suspense into the chapter, carefully delineating the problem before sharing the solution?

This grouping process helps me begin to write sections of an outline and start to order the sections of the chapter. If I have created paragraphs in the chapter itself, I cut and paste my ideas and write a few transitional sentences. I am on my way to filling those blank pages.

Make the central idea the focal point

The key to ordering the puzzle pieces correctly often involves finding that one central piece that helps you place all the others in the right place. In making jewelry, a jeweler will often select one gemstone as the focal point. When I write an outline, I ask myself, what idea is the most important for the message I want to convey? Depending on my organizational pattern, that idea may need to come first, last, or even in the middle of the chapter. Placement of that idea is not about position so much as focus. Every other idea in my chapter will drive attention to that one main concept. Once I choose my central idea, the chapter outline falls into place. Writing the chapter is now as easy as filling in the blanks underneath each section of the outline with supporting details.

For nonfiction writers, a chapter-by-chapter outline is an essential component of the book proposal you will send to publishers. Deep into the publishing process, that outline may help you make structural changes to your book in order to sharpen your message. However important the outline may be to editors, think of that outline as a gift to you. It is your map through the thick forest of your ideas, keeping you from wandering off the path, and safely leading you to your destination. It will help you meet your deadlines on time and keep the ink flowing onto those blank pages. The time you spend writing your outline is an investment. So, go ahead, open the box, dump the puzzle pieces onto your desk, and outline your next book!

SIXTY-EIGHT

Planning for Pansters: Writing a Novel without an Outline

Rachel Phifer

I envy those writers who outline their whole novel before they even begin chapter one. They sit down at their computer, begin typing and already know what they're going to type. A little expansion here, a little fleshing out there. There's no fretting as they try to pick out their story's path one step at a time.

Oh boy, do I wish . . .

But no, I'm a panster (as in I write by the seat of my pants). I've tried outlining, but except for a handful of scenes, I simply cannot tell what needs to happen in a story until I start writing in my characters' voices. One scene leads to the next.

But as J.R.R. Tolkien famously said, "All those who wander are not lost." If you're a panster, trust yourself to discover your novel's path as you write it. A little wandering is likely to give the story a few surprise twists. There are, however, a few tips that will shine a light on your path so that you don't get so far off the track that you have a mess on your hands when you're done.

Keep your premise firmly in mind as you write each scene. It may take you a hundred pages to truly discover where your story is going, but you should have a strong premise from page one, and each scene should build and deepen that premise in some way. Follow tangents as you wish, as long as you keep this in mind, and you'll still have a coherent story in the end.

Before you write, choose two or three comparable novels to the one you intend to write as loose guides. That is, select novels you've read that have the type of structure and audience you're aiming for. The goal isn't to copy other plots, but to give you solid ideas for your story's structure as you go.

Know what your characters' goals are and put obstacles in their way. In every scene. Don't be shy. Stir up the waters and create lots of trouble for your characters. Ultimately, if you write most scenes to make your reader worry, you'll end up with a story that stays on track.

End each scene with a hook. This may simply mean that you've moved your character and his or her goal further apart. But anything that makes your reader want to read on will do (i.e., a mystery that is laid out in the last paragraph). Incidentally, ending on a hook may make it easier for you to know where to start when you come back to the computer as well.

Aim for the finale. Although I don't outline, I generally have a fairly strong image of the catastrophe at the end, that great battle that makes it seem all is lost, but ultimately brings the character to his or her reward. If you know the finale, you'll faithfully build to it.

If you follow these guidelines, you don't need an outline to make sure your story stays on route. But what about coming up with the story itself when you have no outline to refer to?

Last but not least, leave time for your story to stew. If you're not following an outline, you must give your muse time to dream up new scenes. For me, that means taking long walks or doing mindless activities (dishes or laundry) alone, while my mind drifts. When I let my unconscious mind free, I usually find images or snatches of dialogue that will take me through the next scene or two.

SIXTY-NINE

How to Plot by the Numbers

Janalyn Voigt

Show, don't tell. Watch your participial phrases. Don't head hop. Whatever you do, stay within manuscript length recommendations. For a writer scrambling to keep up with all the dos and don'ts, the writing profession can seem full of arbitrary rules. And when someone breaks said rules and goes on to win awards, it's tempting to follow suit. One standard you shouldn't buck, however, is a publishing house's word-length requirements.

Why? Shouldn't you let your story tell itself without regard for its length?

If you will be the one footing the bill, you're free to make your manuscript whatever length you prefer. But if you hope a publisher will pay to produce your book, it's important to understand that additional pages cost extra money, and not just in terms of paper and ink. It takes several editors (who are on the payroll) to review and guide you in polishing a manuscript. Proofreaders don't work for free either. If your last name is Tolstoy or Michener you might get away with submitting a beefy manuscript. The rest of us need to keep the bottom line in mind.

Book stores base the number of copies of a particular title to order on standard widths. If a publisher fails to adhere to these widths, it throws off a bookstore's shelving efforts. Besides this, writing your novel shorter or longer than genre readers expect can negatively influence their buying decisions.

Aren't these considerations crass? What about your inner artist?

Your inner artist will recover, and you'll even grow as a writer from keeping to practical guidelines.

But how on earth can you tell how long a novel will be until you've written it?

You can't know entirely, but I've developed a method that helps me write to a specific length. Even if you're a seat-of-the-pants writer and allergic to plotting, my technique may help you.

1. Estimate your desired word count. If you don't know what that might be, read publishers' submission guidelines at their sites. Find the happy middle ground in a given range. That way you can guard against running too short or too long.

EXAMPLE: A publisher gives the range of 80,000-100,000 words for a historical romance. The middle ground to aim for is 90,000 words.

2. If you already know the average number of words you write per scene, use that figure. If you don't know this number, write the first 50 pages of your book, then estimate the average number of words per scene. You can also base your figures on 1,500 words per scene, but eventually, you'll want to check your own average against this figure and make adjustments as needed. It's okay to round your numbers.

EXAMPLE: Approximately 12,500 / about 8 scenes = 1,500 words per scene

3. Divide your average words per scene into your desired total word count. The answer is the number of scenes to brainstorm.

EXAMPLE: 90,000 / 1,500 = 60 SCENES

4. Develop your plot to include the number of scenes you should write for your desired total word count. Write just a few sentences to describe each scene. This keeps you from bogging down while plotting and gives you a flexible guideline you can easily adjust as you write.

SEVENTY

The Best Advice I (Finally!) 'Got'

Jan Dunlap

I always hated it when writing instructors told me to 1) **write what you know**, and 2) **follow a formula**. How, I wondered, could I write what I knew when I didn't know anything interesting, and when the only formulas I remembered were from high school math class? I was pretty sure that wasn't going to be much help in writing anything other than a final math exam.

Now, having finally decoded those two pieces of cryptic advice in the course of my own writing career development, I have only two words to share with would-be novelists: **read** and **outline**.

Read books (all kinds!), but also **read everything** you can get your hands on: newspapers, magazines, the backs of cereal boxes, newsletters, church bulletins. I even read vanity license plates, which inspired me to give one of my series characters distinctive car plates that have played into more than one mystery plot!

The purpose of all that reading is twofold: 1) you accumulate a storehouse of information about the world; and 2) you never know what word, image, or idea will catch fire in your writing

203

204 | BEST OF WORDSERVE WATER COOLER

process. Reading feeds you with new material—like ongoing brainstorming.

As for reading books in all genres, I find it's a great way to broaden my experience. I may not be an expert on scuba-diving or anti-matter research, or know one end of a knitting needle from the other, but if I've read about it, I at least have some familiarity with it. And if it might fit into something I'm writing, I can go back for more reading or research.

It wasn't until I figured this out—that I didn't have to be an expert about something to write it into a story—that I finally really understood why my teachers insisted you had to 'write what you know.' Write what you know—not necessarily what you yourself have experienced. What a relief to know I didn't have to commit a murder to write about one!

The most important thing I ever did when I was writing my first novel, however, was to outline. And I'm not referring to the outline of my book, either (though I do work from a rough outline when I write). The outline that I found most helpful was the **outline** I made of my **favorite author's best-seller.**

Yes, you read that right—I outlined a book by my favorite author.

It was a tedious task, to be sure, but by the time I finished that chapter-by-chapter outline, I knew more about pacing and plot development than I had ever learned from any teacher or class. My secret was to use a different color marker for each subplot, so that by the end, I had a notebook in which I could visually trace how story threads flowed together and how the notorious 'red herrings' of successful plots operated. Deconstructing a best-selling novel taught me how to write my own 'formula.'

SEVENTY-ONE

The Standalone and the Series

Dianne Christner

Which is better, a standalone novel or a series?
This is a complex question, given each writing career is unique; but here's what I've learned:

Sequel plots evolve naturally.

Most often while writing a novel, an author gets ideas that can spin into sequels. Sometimes minor characters beg for their own stories. Such inspiration is useful in layering the plot of a standalone or planting leads into the first novel of a series.

Most publishers want sequels written six months apart.

This means a solid eighteen months or more of the author's time is contracted. With so many unknowns for a writer, this brings a sense of security. Since the advance represents the entire series, the extra money is valuable upfront for marketing purposes.

Usually less research is needed for a series than subsequent standalone novels, which gives the author extra writing time. With successive deadlines, he is forced to write consistently which also hones his skills and productivity.

Series are popular with publishers unless... the first book doesn't sell.

If the first book doesn't sell, it makes the sequels harder to sell. By the time the author discovers what went wrong, he's probably already into the third book of the series and finds the publisher less willing to spend marketing dollars on the sequels.

For newbies, a series leaves little time for conditioning; you hit the ground running.

The character roster quickly snowballs, yet needs to be worked into the ongoing series. Since each book also stands alone, there is backstory to incorporate. It takes skill to tie it all together. Maintaining consistency makes record-keeping imperative, from character charts to research files. There's a struggle against boredom, and if the author gets bored the reader will too.

Deadlines threaten quality and marketing time.

It's difficult to write quality work with tighter deadlines and also find time to market the *first story* which is the *most important story* for the success of the series. Usually the first story is quite detailed in the original book proposal. But one of the sequels may need major, time-consuming revisions once the editor sees that story evolving.

Why not write a standalone with a series option?

While it sounds like the perfect solution, it's always harder to go down a path when you don't know where it's leading. It's not impossible, but it makes writing the book proposal and novel trickier.

My personal experience—writing a series is like running.

At the beginning, I was excited and fresh. The middle book was written under the most duress. I was struggling uphill because of the increasing time crunch, revisions, and unexpected personal obligations. But the final book was like getting my second wind. It was exhilarating. With writing muscles in peak condition, it was the easiest and most enjoyable to produce. And just beyond beckoned refreshment and reward.

SEVENTY-TWO

Writing a Trilogy

Jordyn Redwood

For those of you starting on your writing journey—there are two realms of publishing. The ABA (the American Booksellers Association) and the CBA (the Christian Booksellers Association). The ABA publishes what are considered secular novels and the CBA publishes Christian or "inspirational" books. Publishers generally fall under one of these two categories.

CBA publishers like trilogies. And there is good reason for this. If you can hook a reader on one, they'll likely buy the rest. There is an inherent marketing value to producing a series. I've not quite seen this trilogy trend in the ABA though there are beloved characters (James Patterson's Alex Cross, Lee Child's Jack Reacher, and Sue Grafton's Kinsey Millhone to name a few) that monopolize more than a few books but are not quite designed as self-enclosed three-book sets.

When my novel *Proof* was first contracted, it was proposed as a trilogy. The publisher didn't like the first proposed sequels and asked for different plot lines in the subsequent titles, which I provided. Even after that, they still contracted only the first. In a twist and turn of God-fingerprinted events, they ended up contracting the trilogy a few months after the initial offer.

However, having not ever written a trilogy, there are a few things I would do now when *planning* a series that I thought could benefit future trilogy authors.

Each book stands alone but should be connected to the others: It's nice for readers if they don't have to read one book to understand the others, but is also nice if certain characters/themes carry through all the books for those sticking with you. This can be challenging because *a little* information will have to be given (in a creative way) to readers to both clue them in to the previous story(ies) and also serve as a nice reminder to those picking up the next book who may have read the others—considering books release six to twelve months apart.

Timelines are important: I know—this should have been uber-obvious to me, right? But consider some things that can seriously mess up your timeline—like characters getting pregnant. You have to then backtrack to the time of conception and make sure all story plots support it. Add to that a hostage story (*Poison*) that deals with younger children that then need to be aged seven years, and a teen pregnancy (yes, I did all of this!) and it can be challenging to make sure all events line up. Graphing out the timeline is a seriously good idea. And then keep it to refer back to until the book is actually in print.

Avoid absolute characterizations: In *Proof,* one character commented that another one never sweats (and it was a blazing hot day and he was in SWAT gear.) It was more to relay how calm the man was under pressure. Well, in *Poison*, my editor reminded me how often this character was now sweating and how I said in book #1 that he never did. It's just like a test—*never, all*, and *always* are not good picks or preludes to character traits.

Provide a circular moment for the reader: What is a circular moment? It's something (an event, an emotion) that happens in the beginning that is revisited at the end of the novel that shows how the character has changed. For instance, in *Proof*, the lead detective, Nathan Long, carries a list of "unforgivables"—acts that he literally writes out that he can't get over emotionally. There is some forgiveness for Nathan at the end of the first book but it ultimately doesn't fully happen until the end of *Peril*, the third book in the series. So each book needs a moment like this as well as the series.

SEVENTY-THREE

Ten Tips for Great Research Interviews

Betsy Duffey and Laurie Myers, The Writing Sisters

You may have heard the advice "Write what you know." But what if you want to write about something you don't know anything about? Find someone who knows. We've interviewed modern day shepherds, airline pilots, engineers, trauma physicians, people from other cultures. Each interview is different and can be valuable in providing the authenticity and detail for your writing. Here are a few tips we've learned.

Start with relationship. Spend some time connecting with your interviewee. Get to know him or her as a person.

Keep questions open ended. Yes-and-no questions don't get you the details you need. Ponder ahead of time what will be the best questions to encourage the interviewee to talk.

Be respectful of boundaries. Let your interviewee determine how much they are comfortable sharing about their personal lives. Don't push, but be ready to go there with them.

Be prepared. Do your homework; learn as much as you can in advance. Search the Internet or read books about the person. We find that the interviews are more productive if we have already written a first draft of the story or chapter. Then we know what blanks to fill in with our expert.

Don't be too structured. Some of the most interesting things we've learned were not from questions on the list. Sometimes, you don't know what to ask.

Don't send advance questions. For an informal interview it's best to explore the subject together. Sending advance questions makes the interviewee focus on your questions rather than the subject.

Listen. Sounds obvious but too often we focus on ourselves and what we are going to say or ask next. Stay focused on what your interviewee is revealing.

Record the session. (We use our cell phones.) Take the focus off of note-taking and trying to remember every detail. You'll be thankful later when you listen to the tape. We've been amazed to find information on the tape that neither of us remembers the interviewee saying.

Respect time. Set an amount of time in advance for the interview and let the person know.

Express thanks. Follow up with a note or email of thanks. You can also bring along a book as a thank you, email a few photos you took, or send a copy of the article or book later when it comes out.

SEVENTY-FOUR

When to Consult a Medical Expert

Jordyn Redwood

Although I've always helped authors along the way with medical questions, it's been one of my primary focuses for the last three years since the invention of Redwood's Medical Edge—my medical blog for authors.

The reason for creating my blog was the multitude of published works I read that were loaded with medical inaccuracies. Not just a few here and there. Time after time, errors caught my eye.

In a podcast interview, the interviewer asked if these medical mistakes would be enough for the average reader to pick up. To be honest, I'm probably more sensitive to these errors after spending 20 years in nursing, but some are mind-numbingly obvious. Such as saying the spleen is on the right side. Such as calling a collar bone a shoulder blade. You don't have to have a medical degree in anything to pick up on these missed anatomy issues.

Writers, I think, are confused as to when it's beneficial to consider consulting a medical expert. And I actually mean more than asking Uncle Joe who has worked as a dentist when you need information about delivering an infant.

Not the best option.

An author who is also a medical expert is your best bet. They know what will overload the reader, they know what is too medically complex for a non-medical author to pull off, and can help you with the nuances (the language and the interactions) since they've worked in the field.

But when is it best to consider plucking down a few hard-earned dollars to work with a medical consultant?

Here are my thoughts.

You need a medical condition that fits a certain set of symptoms. I often get queries from authors along these lines and perhaps they've tried to find something on their own but just cannot decipher the medical language to know, for certain, if it fits: "I need a fatal condition for a child that won't be immediately obvious but could put the child in peril around three months of age." Believe it or not, a metabolic disorder fits this criteria.

You have a medical scenario in mind but aren't sure if it's reasonable. This happens frequently and is probably the most dangerous position to work from. Let's take a look at the following example: "My character has been in a car accident. The car has rolled three times. The injured character was not wearing a seat belt and was thrown 100 yards into a swift moving river, where he almost drowned. He was rescued and required only a minute of CPR to revive him. I need him home from the hospital that night." Or the opposite is true: "I have a character that fell down the stairs and I need him to be in the ICU for three days."

Both of these situations set up implausible medical scenarios. The car accident victim is going to be too injured to go home that day. Someone who requires CPR after nearly drowning is going to be watched, at a minimum, overnight. In order to get admitted into the ICU a patient has to be pretty sick, so the simple fall down the stairs is likely not going to injure the character sufficiently.

Come with an open mind but with a needed result for your character. What I prefer to know is your end game with an open mind to the medical scenario. "I need a character to suffer an injury from a fall that would land them in the hospital for a few days in the ICU and I'm fine with a few extra days in the hospital but I don't want them to have any residual injuries." For you, I would pick an epidural hematoma.

You have a pivotal medical scene. I consulted once for an author who had a child in the Pediatric ICU, dying from leukemia. This is something you want to flow nicely for the reader. If at any moment they pause, look away from the page, and think about the accuracy of what you've written, you've taken them out of the story bubble and perhaps their trust in you has fallen. Perhaps you've even lost a reader.

I once read a review from a fan of historical fiction that skewered an author for writing a completely inaccurate historical scenario in the third book of the series. This reader then doubted the previous two books and swore off reading anything else from the author.

Don't let this happen to you. Consult a medical expert if you find yourself writing these scenarios. It's likely not as expensive as you think.

SEVENTY-FIVE

The Surprising Secret to Juicing Up Your Writing

Anita Agers-Brooks

Sitting at a computer is the place for taking a clunky sentence and smoothing it out, making it read better. I do some of my best writing in my head before I fall asleep for my afternoon nap. I recommend that!
—Tony Hillerman

I don't know about you, but it seems like I spend at least half of my writing time combating fatigue. Maybe it's my crazy on-the-road schedule as a national speaker and business coach. It's possible the myriad of personal problems, some huge, some small, drain my emotions and my body. It could be the anxiety I feel when juggling all of the fine details that go into a professional writing career. Social media—check. Blog—check. YouTube videos—check. Marketing my books—check. Pursue new speaking/coaching gigs—check.

As I view the list, it's no wonder I'm wiped out. But knowing why I'm tired won't change the fact that my books and articles won't write themselves. No one but me can put my words on my pages—the messages I believe God started a burn in my heart to share and show.

But this brings me back to my original problem. What to do when I finally get time to write, but feel too tired to type a word?

The solution is so simple, I'm embarrassed to admit I over-looked it for the longest time. A time-proven technique for juic-ing up your writing. A secret to turning on the creativity, when your muse is turned off.

And here's the secret. Take a short nap.

Sounds crazy, right? But it works. One of the reasons I re-sisted was my fear I'd fall asleep and waste all of that precious time. However, I've found it doesn't happen. Somewhere in the dozing phase, my mind starts whirring with ideas. So much so, after an average of twenty minutes, my inspirations wake me up. Napping has transformed my craft and my process.

I should have known. From the beginning of my writing ca-reer, I've committed and adhered to taking a weekly Sabbath rest. One full day off. No writing. No marketing. No work. It's one of my secret answers to the question I hear so often, "How do you get so much done?"

You see I learned this secret from the Best-Selling Author of all time. God took the first Sabbath, or *shavat vayinafash* in He-brew. The term literally means God rested and got a new soul. And we're meant to live in His image, so why wouldn't we re-new our souls through rest?

I thought, if it works for a whole day, why wouldn't a mini-Sabbath work for part of one? So I tested the theory, and found a twenty-minute nap can infuse me with as much energy as tak-ing a week's vacation. Seriously. It's like gaining an extra day.

Other highly successful authors swear by it. Now I do too.

I believe the quality of my writing has improved from the regular practice of napping, and/or resting in quiet meditation to allow my creative juices freedom to flow. Sabbath renews my soul, clears my mind of clutter, and revives my spirit.

So I challenge you—the next time your eyes droop as you face the keyboard, go against your instincts. Don't push through. Don't beat yourself up. Submit. Give your body the refreshing rest it's crying out for, and feel the juicing begin. Not only will you feel better, but chances are your readers will benefit from your better books.

SEVENTY-SIX

Top Ten Ways to Finish a Book

Kariss Lynch

As I write this, I have just finished up a few days in St. Louis at the ACFW conference. Any other attendees feel like they drank from a fire hose? I'm still digesting all I learned. Still thanking God for orchestrating the meetings He did. As I talked to published and pre-published authors alike, a trend began to emerge.

Those who want it bad enough have the discipline to finish.

Unfortunately finishing doesn't immediately equal a contract. Some pre-published authors have multiple completed manuscripts stuffed in drawers still waiting to be read. To you, I say, "Keep writing and keep pursuing publication!"

To those working on the first book and struggling to finish, life happens. It happens to those with deadlines. It happens to those with contracts.

It happens.

In the publishing world, life revolves around deadlines, and somehow you have to find the will and way to "let your yes be yes" and fulfill your commitment. Editors want to know you can finish and finish well before they invest in you. Before you comment with the specific circumstance that hinders you from finishing that manuscript, let me just say that I get it! And I want to help.

My creativity is officially angled towards my third book now, and as I work to finish that one in the next ten weeks, I can confidently share with you what it took to finish *Shaken* and *Shadowed* and what it will take to finish *Surrendered*.

- Turn off your inner editor and write. I'm not a scientist, but I feel the tug of war in my brain when I try to think technically while thinking creatively. Write. Be creative. Edit later.

- Pick your favorite caffeinated beverage and keep it handy. I became a coffee drinker about a month after I signed my first contract.

- Select a time of day, place, and schedule that works for you! I've tried to become a morning person, but my best writing happens at night. Why fight my body clock? I love to sit in my room or on my patio in the quiet of the night with a candle burning and my creativity racing full speed ahead.

- Alert your cheerleading squad. I have a group of about 20 ladies who consistently ask me about my writing schedule. They know when I have a deadline. They help me process. They are my test subjects when I need a reader's perspective. They see the tears, laughter, creative passion, and the frustration. They know and they encourage me. Find your team.

- Set healthy boundaries. I work full time, write on the side, volunteer in a young adults ministry, have Bible study, and time with friends and family. BALANCE is key.

- Know that life will happen and work around it. This year, I've experienced family emergencies, my brother's wedding, ministry situations, work crises, and somehow the writing gets done. I set my schedule and adjust when necessary. If I miss my word count because of something I can't help, I make it up.
- Cook ahead of time. Don't forget to work out. Take care of yourself! Eating correctly and working out gives you energy to juggle everything.
- Prioritize what's important. For me, it is making sure to focus on the relationships I currently have. The Lord has sovereignly placed me in my city, my family, and my job right now. I need to be present where I am while saying no when necessary to hibernate and write.
- Trust the Lord. He knows your journey. When you feel like nothing is happening, trust that He is working behind the scenes.
- Just do it! Finish strong! You will go from pre-published to publication. But it takes discipline. And chocolate and caffeine. But mostly discipline. And prayer. Tons of that.

SEVENTY-SEVEN

Seven Writing Revelations:
What Blogging Daily throughout Lent Is Teaching Me about Writing

Patty Kirk

Having published five books and taught writing for more years than I want to tot up at this moment, I had no idea I had so much to learn about writing until I undertook, for Lent, to post daily to my blog about following God's command in Deuteronomy 6:7, which is about talking about scripture all the time: when you lie down and get up, when you walk down the road and when you sit in front of the computer.

It's been tough going some days. One night, nigh on midnight, my brother—who has correspondingly committed to responding to my daily posts—sent me an email reminding me that I still hadn't posted that day. Mostly, though, blogging about the Bible daily has proved a blessed Lenten entertainment—much more fun than giving something up—and taught me much about writing discipline.

Here's what I've learned so far.

It *is* possible to write daily.

Or, so far it is, anyway. Previously I had doubted this.

I had the same revelation once about dieting and lost thirty pounds. The sad news is that, as with most of my spiritual revelations, I forgot what I had learned and gained a lot of it back.

(Note to self: After Lent, instead of blogging daily, you need to track what you eat.)

One key to discipline in writing is writing on a set schedule.

I've found I have the best chance of getting my blogwork done if I do it first thing in the morning, before the day has the chance to talk me out of it. It's the same way with my running: I either do it in the morning or I don't do it at all. Similarly, as with my 21-miles-per-week running commitment, the once-a-day blogging mandate has a sort of built-in incentive: incremental progress toward success. When I get done with my day's post or run, accomplishment surges through my veins and arteries. *Yes!* I tell myself.

Daily writing is easier if you follow a chronology of some sort.

This is by no means the first time I have tried to force myself to blog regularly, though in the past my goal has been to blog not daily but only (blush) weekly. I have never gotten very far with it. Even with a clear topical focus (which helps), eventually I just lose a sense of forward movement and stop.

This time around, though, I have not only a topic but a predetermined chronology: Jesus' biographical development as presented in the four accounts of it in Matthew, Mark, Luke, and John. I started—following a more occasional trajectory— back at Christmastime. Something about there being a passage of time in the material I'm reading and responding to flings me forward, I think, by providing me with an unknown element to look forward to. I wake up in the morning curious about what's going to happen next in Jesus' life—and how thinking about it might play out in mine.

Blogging is work.

As pleasurable as it has been to read and think about and respond to scripture every morning, not very long after I committed to daily blogging I started to think of it as work. As, that is, something I was *supposed* to accomplish by the end of the day. A duty. At times a burden. And always, potentially, an additional stressor I don't need in my life. This is a reality that I can't afford to ignore.

Time devoted to blogwork takes away from time devoted to other writing.

As with all work, every minute I spend blogging is a minute I'm not working on my other writing projects. This is another reality I can't afford to ignore.

One of these days publishers will discover how blogging saps writing—or, that is, they will admit it to be true, having tried regular blogging themselves—and they will, I'm certain, start discouraging their authors from regular blogwork. (I am prophesying here.)

Before that happens, however, publishers may cease to exist. (Another prophecy.)

Habitual blogwork on something different from your main writing project can help your creativity.

While blogging has cost me time I need for the novel I'm working on, allowing myself to concentrate on something else for a portion of my designated writing days has also unstopped the writer's block I tend to have when writing fiction. This is partly so, I think, because I am, in essence, transferring some of the duty and burden of regular writing onto the blog and off of my novel, making the latter more of a place to just have fun.

It is important to note, too, that creativity studies consistently show that turning one's attention to something else—something unrelated—invariably nurtures creativity.

Having a dependable and responsive reader—or better yet, readers!—is a wonderful incentive to keep the words coming.

As I said at the start, when I committed to read scripture and blog about it daily, my brother committed to read and respond to what I wrote. Not only have these responses proved a lovely opportunity to interact daily with a faraway loved one, but my brother's insights have grown me. Often, in fact, his responses have triggered the next day's post. Best of all, we talk to each other daily about scripture, which was the goal of my blog in the first place: to be in conversation with others about scripture all the time.

I'm certain there are more things I will learn from my daily blogging commitment—and probably more things that I have learned already—but seven's a good number, so I'll let this be enough for now. I need to get on to daily blogging—and, after that, the novel!

VII.

Revising and Editing

SEVENTY-EIGHT

How to Edit a Manuscript

Kariss Lynch

You've edited a paragraph, a chapter, maybe a few chapters, but now your manuscript is ready to go and your editor sent you back the first round of edits full of major content changes. Where do you begin?

Editing the manuscript as a whole can seem like a daunting task. Editing is a necessary evil to me. I prefer writing any day. But I'm always pleased with the end result after time spent editing.

The truth is that editing needs to be a matter of prayer before you feel tempted to knock your computer off the desk. (Kidding. Kind of.) It can feel frustrating and detailed and confining after a fluid writing process to finish your book.

Here's the good news: If you crafted your story correctly, it should be frustrating. Just look at it as a challenge to overcome. Content edits often include tweaking details used in major story lines. You have to track each story line down and make sure your changes are consistent. If you tweak one detail, it may cause you to slightly amend a detail in another story line. I was thankful to see that my story lines were so interwoven that one change affected another but was terrified I would miss something. But don't worry, that's where your editor comes in to catch anything you missed. Just try to do your due diligence on the front end.

I just finished a round of edits for my second book, *Shadowed*. Here are some of my takeaways for a major content edit:

1) Start small.

Read through ALL of the suggestions from your editor. Weigh what she is asking. Then set the manuscript aside for a couple of days. Process the best way you can tackle the job. Pray that you will know the parts to keep and parts to cut, when to kill your darlings and when to fight.

2) Make a plan.

I found it difficult to keep scrolling through the manuscript to find all the places I needed to fix, especially when it came to juggling scenes and chapters for better time placement. Write down a knock list and cross out each item as your finish it. You will feel accomplished and know you are moving in the right direction. Even if the list is extensive, take it one step at a time. If something else comes to mind, write it down and come back to it. You can do this!

3) Take your first pass.

Start at the top and work through until THE END. Write down any questions you may have about research or editor comments. Make all the smaller changes you can make right away. For instance, I noticed I referred to an organization two different ways in my manuscript. For consistency's sake, I used the "Find and Replace" feature in Word for an easy fix to ensure accuracy. Easy check mark on my list!

4) Attack the major problems with gusto.

It helped me to print my manuscript, make notes, and then get to work. My editor suggested some things that I struggled to pull off. However, when I looked at a clean, printed manuscript, I was able to take her suggestions with my preferences and style and make the changes something that fit the story better. I love to work with my hands, so it helped to have something to hold and mark up with a pen. It also got me time away from my computer screen, which gave me a great brain break.

5) Finish strong and pray.

Time for that final look. I try to make it my goal to tackle as many issues as possible so the next edit is easier. Send the editor any notes she may need to do her job well and help you. I learned on my last edit that sending an accompanying timeline saves LOADS of time for both you and the editor.

Finish by praying that God will use this for the process ahead and that the finished product will bring God glory. Take a deep breath, type that email, and click send. Your manuscript is changing, but so are you!

SEVENTY-NINE

Editing Tips

Henry McLaughlin

Books aren't written, they're rewritten. Including your own. It is one of the hardest things to accept, especially after the seventh rewrite hasn't quite done it . . .
—Michael Crichton

The workshop leader looked over the group—a motley crew of aspiring and published authors seeking to learn. She arched her eyebrow and said, "The purpose of your first draft is to get the crap out. Then you can go back and write the book." Okay, I thought, that's an interesting way to look at it. And it actually freed me to write better.

I've also learned that each draft has crap in it. The goal is to have less and less in each revision. Even today, I'll pick up my published novel, *Journey to Riverbend,* and see things I would change. And the published version is the eighth draft.

Over the years, people have asked me, "What's the best way to edit?"

I don't think there is one best way to edit. Each writer will develop his own way of editing, mostly though trial and error.

My editing process has evolved as I've written more, studied the craft, and learned to test approaches and keep the ones that work.

When I write, I begin the day by reading what I wrote the day before. I look for typos, adverbs, passive tense, glaring POV

231

issues, and grammar. This also helps me get back into the flow of the story.

On Saturday, I print out the pages for that week and do a deep edit of the week's writing, polishing and refining, cutting scenes, re-working dialogue, correcting inconsistencies from the plot or character.

I use critique partners and group as I'm working on the story, incorporating their input as I go along.

Once the first draft is finished, I put it away. For a minimum of three weeks. If any thoughts come to me about the book, I put them in a folder until later. I send the story out to beta readers. At this point, I find I need at least two people to read the entire book and give me feedback to specific questions.

After three weeks, I pull out the manuscript and have my computer read it to me. And then I rewrite the story, incorporating input from the beta readers.

The second draft goes through almost the same process as the first, generally more quickly. And then it gets rewritten.

Editing is kind of like washing your hair—lather, rinse, repeat. Over and over.

There are two books I think are immensely helpful in this process: *Self-editing for Fiction Writers* by Renni Browne and Dave King. And, *Write Great Fiction: Revision and Self-Editing* by James Scott Bell.

EIGHTY

The Warp and Woof of Weaving Stories

Jan Dunlap

When I was in college, I went on a retreat. One of the skills I learned during the weekend was basket weaving. It was a lovely art, both in what I ended up with, and how I got there. In other words, the process led to a product I was proud of: a tightly woven basket with an intricate design of my own creation.

Writing a novel, I find, parallels that experience. The warp of my story is the primary structure, and the woof is the way I hold it together by weaving in and out of the structure with the scenes and details that make it distinctly my own design. Sometimes, I make an impulsive change in the course of the weaving of my tale, which then affects the entire design, and I end up with a different—but even better—story than I had anticipated; sometimes, I find the change is a mistake, which means I have to unravel back to that point and make corrections.

Unlike crafting a basket, however, the task of weaving a story gives me a dimension of creativity the basket doesn't allow: I can add in even more layers—more woof—after my initial story is complete. When I finish a basket, the weaving is of one piece—I can't cut out a section of threads and replace it, or expand it, and expect the basket to hold together.

With writing, though, I find the extra woof is what gives the story its defining success. In revision, I can add a new character to further complicate the plot or add comic relief. While the main structure of the work doesn't change, that new character can help breathe more interest into interactions with, and between, other characters. In the case of my mysteries, I often create a character in the revision process who can help move my story through spots that are weak or slow, especially when I need some red herrings thrown in to mislead my readers. I created one such character in my first book as a last-minute thought to complement one of the subplots, only to have readers so enjoy the character, that they repeatedly asked me to bring him back in a later book!

Adding in subplots that reflect the primary plot is another trick to elaborating on my initial story design. When revising, I try to give almost every character some personal issue that can tie into another character's. Doing so not only makes the characters more real—who, in real life, doesn't have problems to deal with?—but it affords me more opportunities to weave in conflict, which adds to the story's pacing. My solution to keeping track of the characters and subplots is the creation of a master flow chart that follows each element of the story from beginning to end. That way, I accomplish every weaver's goal: no loose ends.

Happy weaving!

EIGHTY-ONE

Seven Tips for Self-Editing Your Novel

Melissa K. Norris

Before I signed with my agent, I knew my novel needed another round of edits. I looked at several freelance editors, but I just couldn't afford the cost. So, I rolled up my shirt sleeves, prayed, and decided to do it myself. Again.

At this point, I'd already gone through my book for grammatical errors, typos, etc. I'd had a published writer and several beta readers go through it. Three other agents expressed interest if I could go back and make my novel stronger.

Here are the tips I learned that pushed my book from a maybe to yes.

1. Print it out. I fought this (don't ask me why, my frugalness I suppose, sounds better than stubbornness), but it truly makes a huge difference. Your eye will catch things on the printed page you won't see on the computer screen.

2. Only edit one thing at a time. Go through your manuscript focusing on one thing at a time. Do a sweep for dialogue. Is there useless chatter? Talking that doesn't move the story forward? Do you have too many tags? Then go back for description. And so forth.

3. Examine every character. Don't waste time with cardboard characters or the stereotypical bad guy. I highly recommend Deb Dixon's *Goal Motivation and Conflict*.

4. Setting. Regardless if you write historical or contemporary, you need to research your setting. Find some of the not so common places to set your characters in. For example, lots of scenes are in restaurants, change it up and put them on a picnic at some fantastic landmark.

5. Hooks and cliff-hangers. Check out the beginning of every chapter and the ending. What can you do to make it stronger? What could happen that would ensure the reader couldn't put your book down because they have to know what happens next? Is your heroine being chased by a wolf? Then make it a pack of wolves and have her twist her ankle. Take it a step further and do this to every scene. I recommend James Scott Bell's *Revision and Self-Editing*.

6. Description. Remember to include things beyond sight. Let us know how it smells, tastes, feels, and sounds. Is the rain splattering or pounding? Are the hero's hands calloused or warm?

7. Wrapping up all the ends. Make sure all the sub-plots and story lines are resolved. You can set things up for a sequel, but you can't leave things undone. Readers will feel cheated if they have to buy the next book to find out what happens to the main storyline in book one.

EIGHTY-TWO

Editing: Pay Now or Pay Later

Bob Welch

It happens every time. OK, nearly every time.

I unwrap the book-size package and am soon holding the dream-come-true from one of our Beachside Writers workshop students: the memoir that they've worked on for years, finally out.

I'm so proud of them. And, a few pages into it, so wishing they had found an editor—or four. Because as I read along, I am suddenly jolted by by an extra word. Or by four spaces after a period instead of one. Or by a writers' negligence in putting an apostrophe in the wrong place.

You get the idea.

If you're going to invest the time, energy and money into a book, be willing to invest in a good editor.

Even then, your book will still have errors. All of my twenty books have had errors. Any time flawed human beings have their manuscripts edited by flawed human beings, imperfection is assured. Still, discipline yourself, humble yourself and bring in others to create the cleanest book you can.

Why *doesn't* that happen?

- By the time you get to the final edit of a book, you're so physically tired and mentally drained that any goals of perfection fell by the wayside three meltdowns ago.

- Your eyes are so focused on the finish line—*I just want this thing done*—that you miss the barriers right in front of you. Editing/fact-checking a book is the literary equivalent of running track and field's steeplechase event: in your deepest fatigue, you still have to jump barriers—and splash into a water pit—lap after lap.
- You can't afford—or aren't willing to pay for—an editor.
- You can't find such an editor.
- You subconsciously know an editor will find lots of errors and you can't take the humiliation.

I get it. This is not the fun part. But here are some solutions:

- Go into it with your eyes open, understanding that when you're done with a second or third draft, you're not nearly done. I remember building a kitchen add-on, my first project of this caliber. When I had the space all framed in, I famously said, "Almost done now!" A contractor friend politely pointed out that I wasn't even half done. Trim work takes way longer than you think.
- Edit and fact-check along the way so there's less to do at the end. It takes discipline, I know. But every weed you don't pluck by hand in April is a field of weeds you need to take a gas-powered string trimmer to come August. Put another way: better to floss regularly than think you can go at it diligently the night before your cleaning appointment—and fool your dentist.
- When setting up long-range deadlines for the book, leave ample time for editing your manuscript yourself and bringing in others to help. Yes, that's *others*, as in

more than one. I've had up to six people read my manuscripts before I send them to the publisher. My reasoning? Pay now or pay later. I'd rather be humiliated midway through the process in front of a few people than embarrassed at the end in front of thousands.

- Hire a professional editor if possible. If not, seek out friends and acquaintances who you think will do a good job. They needn't be writers themselves, though, of course, that's a plus. But, for my needs, they need to be "detail" people who know language, play well with others and, amid their surgical incisions, put on an occasional happy face to remind me I'm not a total loser.

- To find an editor, start talking to people. Editors are hard to find; it's not like ordering a pizza. But if you just start talking, texting and e-mailing people, you'll find someone.

- Be willing to spend some money. I'm always amazed at the number of writers who cringe at the idea of paying someone to edit their manuscript. And yet they'd pay someone to mow their lawn, clean their gutters or change the oil in their car. I generally pay someone $100 to $500, depending on the project. I also have friends who refuse to accept money, and who wind up with gift certificates or a dinner out instead. But to not *expect* to pay someone is to undervalue the worth of your project—and their time.

- Consider going the print-on-demand route. I call it "grace personified." You have chance after chance to be forgiven the errors of your ways, in that you can make fix after fix once the book is initially released.

You'll never produce a perfect book. And that's OK. We're imperfect people. But at least put in the effort—and perhaps money—to try.

EIGHTY-THREE

Revising Aloud

Patty Kirk

R eading aloud," I'm always telling my writing students, "is the best way to revise."

I encourage them—sometimes require them—to find read-aloud partners or start writing groups in which they take turns reading their work aloud.

"Hearing your sentences spoken lets you know whether they're clear and natural-sounding—whether someone actually *could* speak them," I explain. "And it doesn't work to read to an empty room. You need a warm body, a listener, to complete the communication. Speaking is, after all, a collaborative act."

Finding that read-aloud partner is easy at college, where everyone's engaged in writing all the time. Outside the college setting, though, finding someone willing to listen can be a challenge. People are busy. Few have time to sit still for an hour while some verbose writer drones on. That's how they'll imagine it when you propose reading to them. We Americans have lost—or never had—the habit of listening to people read. We had only the shallowest tradition of serial novels, released chapter by chapter as Dickens' novels were and read to the whole family at fireside. And no comfy pubs—without blaring TVs— like the one where C. S. Lewis, J. R. R. Tolkien, and their writer buddies hung out, drank beer, and read their work to one another. Writers who give public readings these days will tell you it's hard to get even close friends to attend. Our lives are too busy for read-alouds.

I often recommend to writer friends that they make use of the lonely people in their lives: shut-in relatives, kid-imprisoned friends who wish they had a grownup to talk to, recently retired colleagues with time on their hands.

It sounds terrible, this "making use" of others, taking advantage of their neediness to assuage your own, but in my experience such mutual exchanges not only helped my writing but also transformed intended acts of mercy—"I should spend more time with my mother-in-law," I was always telling myself—into pleasurable time together, which we both looked forward to. My mother-in-law not only got longed-for company but also felt needed; I got my warm body but also genuine enjoyment, without having to chide myself (usually in vain) to, as Paul recommends, "give what you have decided in your heart to give, not reluctantly or under compulsion, for God loves a cheerful giver" (2 Corinthians 9.7 NRSV). The mutual benefit, I found, guaranteed that cheerfulness, for both of us—because attentive listening and being listened to can't help but nurture relationships.

My daughter Lulu has been on semester break from college for the past month, with a couple more weeks to go. It's tricky having a grown daughter home that long. We've long since put our Christmas CDs away, but I'm still in the throes of Bing Crosby's parental prophecy for the season: "And Mom and Dad can hardly wait for school to start again!"

Luckily, Lulu's engrossed in the final revision stages of her senior project—a hundred-page translation of and critical introduction to an East German book—and I'm busy trying to cut 30,000 words from a novel before sending it out, so we have tasks to distract us from the inevitable mother-daughter combat. Also, since we're in about the same place in our revisions—where what we need most is to hear them aloud and find out if they work—we've established a read-aloud schedule: I read her a couple short chapters during her late breakfast, and she reads me one long chapter while I trim vegetables for dinner.

I can't say it's the perfect exchange my mother-in-law and I had. Lulu doesn't end my readings, as my mother-in-law always did, with "That's the best thing you've ever written!" And, as a writer and teacher of writing, I give more critical feedback than Lulu really wants. But our reading fills two hours of our day with mostly pleasurable, mutually beneficial work. More importantly, the listening involved gives us both practice, at this complex juncture of our parental-filial journey, in navigating our new relationship as related but separate adults. As peers, in other words. Equals. Reciprocally heard, appreciated, and loved.

EIGHTY-FOUR

To Write a Book Someday, Share Your Writing Now

Lisa Velthouse

Some people will tell you the defining characteristic of a writer is that he or she is someone who writes. There is truth to that perspective, but it fails to offer a complete picture. It also gives many "aspiring writers" an excuse to be nothing more than journal keepers: diligently plucking away at Moleskine memoirs or first-novel manuscripts that have zero chance of getting published, ever.

The point here is not a matter of quality. It's about privacy.

The reason why many written works-in-progress will never see the light of publishing day is that they are stowed, always and forever, in a drawer or on a hard drive where they have no risk of being evaluated by a second person. The writers of these works will never be writers because they will never have readers. They exist completely outside the writing market, and the only critical eye they allow to view their work is their own.

If you think that one day you'd like for people to read your writing, then you should begin by inviting people to read your writing now. Here are five ways readers can strengthen your writing and make it even more worth reading:

Readers help you get over yourself. It's not uncommon for writers to feel uncertain or insecure about what they've written. *Will this technique work here? Am I being clear? Am I using a marketable concept? Does anybody else care about the subject?* Without readers to help confirm where and how a piece of writing is hitting its target (and where and how it's missing its mark), these uncertainties and insecurities often grow and fester. But when you prioritize feedback, typically you get it. As a result you might find that your sinking suspicions will be confirmed. Some of your assumptions might be challenged. Maybe you'll be pleasantly surprised by rave reviews. Whatever the case, you won't be stuck wondering anymore, and that will help light a clear way forward.

Readers identify strengths in your work. Encouragement and affirmation give extra fuel when you're trying to produce a manuscript. So ask your readers to note the places where they laugh out loud, hold their breath with anticipation, get caught by surprise, can't stop turning pages, or are struck speechless. That paragraph you're thinking about deleting? It might be your readers' favorite part. Give them a chance to tell you so.

Readers identify weaknesses in your work. That poetic metaphor you've taken days and months to craft? It might be so complex that it's confusing your readers. The story you've built a whole chapter around? Your readers might be bored out of their minds.

As the writer of a work, you will undoubtedly feel more attached to it than your readers will. Because of your heightened emotional attachment, you'll probably miss seeing some of your writing's flaws. You might even be blind to enormous holes in the work. Let your readers open your eyes to the problems you don't see, so you can take the opportunity to fix them.

Readers expand your perspective. You are only one person, so your outlook on the world is limited and skewed. You have strange views about certain things, and some of your views simply haven't been challenged in a way that forces you to clarify them well or charitably. Readers can help you identify the odd little points in a draft, the ones that either are or seem arrogant, stingy, dismissive, hyper-emotional, you name it. Points like these will jut out in unseemly ways, always subtracting and distracting from good work, unless someone will be so kind as to call your attention to them, so you can know to improve them.

Readers make the process realistic. If your writing aspirations are real, then you're going to have to accept the reality of readers at some point. Get used to feedback now, and critiques won't make you crazy later. Write with readers in mind now, and it won't feel strange when they're a part of the process later. Start learning what readers are interested in now, and then when your defining moments as a writer come, you'll be prepared to deliver for your readers.

EIGHTY-FIVE

What Is a Beta Reader, and Why Do We Need Them?

Sharon A. Lavy

How exciting. Your manuscript is finished. You have edited it. Had it critiqued by writers you respect. Possibly even had it edited by a freelance editor. It's time to shoot it off to your agent or publisher. Right?

Not so fast. Your grammar may be immaculate. Every i is dotted, every t is crossed, and you are sure you watched your ps and qs. But don't forget the most important part of the process. The beta reader.

Dear Reader of my novel . . ,

What does an author expect/hope for from a beta reader? The story resides in my mind for so long that I reach a point when I need readers to tell me if I've said what I think I have. You are a very important part of the editing process. If you feel your suggestion can make the book better, easier to read, and more understandable, please elaborate.

1. Did the prologue and/or first chapter make you want to read more?

2. At the end of each chapter, were there unanswered questions that made you want to flip the page and keep reading?

3. Did you relate to any of the characters? Did you see character development in the major characters? Which character needs more work?

4. Did you stay interested until the end? Where did your interest lag?

5. Did you find a place where you were confused? Help me find and fix that.

6. Did the ending give closure? Do you feel it satisfied the needs of the story?

7. Is this a book you could recommend to your reading friends?

8. Did you recognize a spiritual thread running through the book? Too much? Not enough? Explain.

9. Did you find any plot holes that need to be fixed? A scene that doesn't fit with this version of the story? (This happens in editing when we delete a subplot but don't catch all the loose threads of the no-longer-needed part of the story.)

As an author, I need to know more of the story than I put on the page. This helps me know the characters and why they act as they do. But it might not belong in *this* story.

As a beta reader, try to look at the big picture. If you see typos, feel free to note them, but don't worry if you miss them at this stage of the game. Thank you. You are valuable and I appreciate you.

What type of person makes the best beta reader? The answer to that question is: "It depends." Common wisdom says not to ask your relatives. Common wisdom says to ask a reader of the genre you write. Each author will learn by trial and error.

Who was the first beta reader I asked to read my latest manuscript? My brother-in-love. A man who doesn't read fiction.

Why? Because he read my first book, read every word. Pointed out important plot holes, and recommends my book to others.

By the way, he still doesn't read fiction. He prefers "real" books. But he offers to read mine because he has so much fun finding the plot holes.

EIGHTY-SIX

Cutting Out the Frivolous Stuff

Patty Kirk

Last week, during a series of presentations on writing-related discoveries, which I always make first-year composition students do at the end of the year, one student said, "I learned that writing shorter is harder than writing longer."

"Why's that, do you think?" I asked.

He thought before answering.

"Because to make something shorter, you have to make all these decisions. Like, what's important and what to get rid of. And then, after you take stuff out, you have to change other stuff to make it sound right."

"You mean, you have to revise—like, you know, re-see it," another student chimed in.

"Yeah. It *is* like that," he said. "Like seeing that it could be a different way and still be what I wanted to say. Maybe even better. I never thought of that. I always used to think revision was just fixing stuff." The two students grinned with that mixture of embarrassment and pride students always have when using the language of the course.

That night I led a professional development session for graduate faculty on the subject of assessing final projects.

"Everything students hand in is a draft," I remarked in passing, "and drafts are hard to grade. If you want your students to revise, you have to trick them into it."

"How?" one professor asked.

"Lots of ways," I said, "but the most successful way for me is to give maximum word limits on assignments rather than minimum word limits."

"How does that make them revise?" she persisted.

I knew that being made to write short did force students to revise, but it took me a second to come up with a reason why on the spot. "I guess it's like when you fill out an online application and have to answer a question in a little box that limits you to only so many characters, including spaces," I told them. "What you write is always way too long. So you have to keep paring it down, getting rid of unnecessary stuff, often the parts you're proudest of, so you can get down to what's essential. And, in the end, it's not only shorter but better. Or, anyway, I always think it is. In my experience, the same thing happens with students when I give them word limits. I get all these emails, begging me to let them go longer. But I never do. Not one word. So they have to revise. And what they turn in is lots better than what they turn in when they're just trying to fill pages."

Everyone wrote that down—the most useful grading takeaway, even though it wouldn't be relevant until they started building assignments the next semester.

The next day, at an end-of-year luncheon of honors English students, my department chair asked those about to graduate to share the moment they realized they wanted to study English, and two women talked about learning to write short.

"Being forced to cut made my writing so much better," one said. "I knew how to improve my writing after learning that."

"I had this revelation that every sentence matters," said another. "That was the moment for me."

Finally, yesterday, my novel workshop students were talking about their revision strategies for the three chapters I'd be grading at the end of the semester.

"I'm cutting out a lot of frivolous stuff," one said. "That's the main thing I learned in this class: You don't need half the stuff you write."

As always, whenever I have one of these clumps of similar messages, I figured it wasn't just coincidence—or the more obvious reality that people were saying back to me what I'd been preaching all semester—but the Holy Spirit weighing in on the subject. It seemed strange, though, that the Holy Spirit was interested in revision.

Then it occurred to me that I'm the one who needed the cutting message I'd been preaching. My own novel is a frivolous (and practically unpublishable for a first novel) 130,000 words.

There's no getting around it, I told myself. *You need to cut another 30,000 words.*

That doesn't begin to answer the question—if you're still wondering—of why cutting words from my pages might interest the Holy Spirit. Perhaps it's that, as I like to tell my students, revision is a key part of the creative process, and God has always been into that. Separating light from dark, water from land. Fiddling with it, examining it, considering, until it's good, or very good.

Or maybe God's interested in revision for the same reason he pays attention to sparrows: namely, all of his creation—birds, us, our minds, words, our little improvement plans—fascinates and delights him.

EIGHTY-SEVEN

Rewriting: Seven Simple Tips

Betsy Duffey and Laurie Myers, The Writing Sisters

When we started *The Shepherd's Song*, the ideas came fast and the words flowed. We didn't stop that precious flow by asking ourselves questions. Our mother had taught us that. Get the words down, then you can shape them and refine the writing.

Here are some tips for rewriting, and some examples from the first chapter of *The Shepherd's Song*.

1. <u>Stick to what the character is personally experiencing</u>.

FIRST DRAFT: *The ambulance doors opened and Kate's stretcher was pulled out of the back. The wheels hit the ground and they were inside within seconds. Doctors and nurses surrounded her, each performing a different task, all with the goal of saving her life.*

This first draft tells us what is happening. We hear the voice of a narrator. But if the scene is from Kate's POV, we want to show the reader only what she is experiencing. Here's the rewrite:

FINAL DRAFT: *She felt jarred as the stretcher was pulled forward, then lights and swirls of snow. The wheels hit the ground and they were inside within seconds. Masked faces in white and green hovered over her. Gloved hands touched her.*

2. <u>Do a search for the word "thought." See if you need it</u>.

FIRST DRAFT: *A brief memory of her car plowing into another vehicle flashed across her mind. 'A car accident,' she thought. 'I've been in a car accident.'*

Extra words take the reader out of the character's head. There's no need to tell the reader that the character is thinking. Just say it.

FINAL DRAFT: *A brief memory came—her car sliding on the slick road, the sound of breaking glass and crunching metal. A car accident.*

3. Limit speech tags.

FIRST DRAFT: *"What happened?" the young man doing the CT scan asked.*

"Car accident," the nurse said. "A big pile-up on I-95."

"No kidding. She doesn't look so good. Is she going to make it?" he asked, helping them roll Kate into the room.

"Too early to tell," Dr. Belding said.

The nurse shrugged. "You never know with these trauma patients. I've seen ones in worse shape make it, but not many. If I were the kind to bet, I'd bet 'no' for this woman."

"Too bad," the young man said.

Can you see how awkward this is? The tags (he said, she said), are slowing down the action and are reminding us that it is a written story.

FINAL DRAFT: *She heard the voices back and forth over her stretcher.*

"What happened?"

"A big pile-up on I-95. Twenty-five cars, six semis and one bus."

"No kidding. She doesn't look so good. Is she going to make it?"

"You never know with these trauma patients. I've seen ones in worse shape make it ... but not many."

Kate closed her eyes again. I might die.

Here's another place we rewrote, removing the tag.

FIRST DRAFT: *He picked up the receiver and said, "This is John McConnell."*

FINAL DRAFT: *He fumbled for a moment with the receiver, then got it to his mouth with shaking hands. "This is John McConnell."*

Having a checklist for rewrites is helpful and a quick way to review a manuscript. Using search features allows us to quickly find and replace words like "thought" or "said."

4. <u>Watch out for the word "felt" when describing a character's feelings.</u> Remember the old saying: show don't tell.

FIRST DRAFT: *She felt confused and out of control.*

This is okay for a first draft but needs rewriting.

FINAL DRAFT: *"What's your name?"*

She tried to focus. Her name?

"Kate . . . McConnell." She gasped out each word.

"Your birthday?"

She tried to come up with the answer, but it was too confusing. Tears welled up.

"It's all right. Just stay with me."

"What hap...?" She wanted to finish the sentence but could not.

5. <u>Eliminate prepositional phrases that tell us about the character or action.</u>

FIRST DRAFT: *Without hesitation the nurses joined Dr. Belding in pushing the stretcher toward the elevators.*

Instead of telling the reader "without hesitation," why not put the scene in play and show them?

FINAL DRAFT: *Dr. Belding grabbed the end of the stretcher. "Okay, people. Let's get her down to the OR." He turned to the nurse. "Has the family been called?"*

6. <u>Watch out for the word "saw."</u> Show us what the character is seeing instead.

FIRST DRAFT: *He slipped the phone out of his pocket and saw the text message from his dad.*

We don't need to explain that the character saw something. Show it from the character's POV.

FINAL DRAFT: *Matt slipped the phone out of his pocket.*

'Emergency. Call me.'

A text from his dad. That was unusual.

7. <u>Evaluate each adverb</u>. Is there a better way to show the reader what is happening?

FIRST DRAFT: *John McConnell looked up in irritation at his secretary.*

"I said hold all calls," he said impatiently.

Telling reminds the reader that it is not real. Staying in the character's head means we show through the character's actions what is happening, and how they are feeling. We had to rewrite to show his impatience.

FINAL DRAFT: *"Mr. McConnell. A phone call, line three." His secretary spoke from the doorway.*

"I said to hold all calls." He continued scanning the document in front of him.

"I know, but."

"I am well aware that we all need to get out of here."

EIGHTY-EIGHT

The Search-and-Find Feature

Barbara Scott

Over the years I've harped at authors never, ever to turn in a first draft. Some writers think the editor's job is to spiff up their grammar, correct misspelled words, change passive voice to active, eliminate repeated words and phrases, or do laser surgery on their mixed metaphors.

Word travels in publishing circles about whether you're a professional or you've made your living on the backs of good editors. You don't want to be known as a hack writer.

Hopefully, the electronic tool known as search and find or search and replace will make your self-editing chore more enjoyable.

1. Passive voice (one of my pet peeves): Passive voice is created by using a form of the verb *to be*, such as *am, is, are, was, were, being, be,* or *been* and followed by the past participle of the main verb, or gerunds comprised of a present participle (ending in "ing") that functions as a noun. Learn more in Hacker's *Rules for Writers.* Search for these words and recast (rewrite) your sentences to make them more active. Examples:

Passive: He was jumping off the cliff into the river below to escape.

Active: He jumped off the cliff into the river below to escape.

2. Qualifiers: These words clutter up your writing. Sometimes I think writers use them to boost their word counts. Examples: *begin, start, started to, almost, decided to, planned to, a little bit, almost,* etc. Examples:

   With qualifier: Mary felt a little bit out of place among the *nouveau riche.*

   Better: Mary felt out of place among the *nouveau riche.*

3. Weasel Words: These words are easy to spot. You can drop them and no one will ever notice. Mark Twain once said, "Substitute 'damn' every time you're inclined to write 'very'; your editor will delete it and the writing will be just as it should be."

   Other examples include *really, well, so, a lot of, anyway, just, oh, suddenly, immediately, kind of, extremely,* etc. I'm sure you can come up with your favorites.

   With weasel words: Suddenly, she stood up and said, "Oh well, let's retire to the drawing room and just stay out of his way."

   Better: She stood. "Let's retire to the drawing room and stay out of his way."

4. Adverbs: I don't hate adverbs, but they "usually" are unnecessary, especially in dialogue tags. Your prose should

communicate a character's state of mind without using a tag line such as the example below. Use search and find to look for an *ly* followed by a space or a period.

With adverb: "I'll kill him," she said ferociously. (Really?)
Better: "I'll kill him!"

5. Extraneous *thats* or *thens*: Use the global search-and-find feature for the word *that*. If you can understand the sentence without the word, you don't need it. You notice I didn't write, *then* you don't need it. Both of these words are over used.

Writing is rewriting, and rewriting involves self-editing. It's your job to turn in the cleanest manuscript possible to your agent or editor. Use the search-and-find tool or the search-and-replace feature to speed up the process.

EIGHTY-NINE

A Word Miser's Experience with Line Edits

Katie Ganshert

I have two confessions.

I hold tightly to my words.

And of all the things that lay ahead as a contracted author, line-edits made me the most nervous.

Here's my truth. I'm in love with words. I love stringing them together in creative and clever ways to paint pictures for the reader. I don't like deleting them. And I'm super protective of my voice.

So the idea of line-editing scared me.

I admitted all this to my incredibly talented line-editor, Lissa Johnson, and she said it's a common malady for writers, especially beginners. Which makes sense if you think about parenting. We tend to be much more uptight with our firstborn, don't we?

So how did line-edits go? Did I have to get rid of words I wanted to keep? Does the writing still sound like me? Was it as painful as I feared? Is the story better?

Good. Yes. Yes. Yes (but not in the way I expected). Very much.

Allow me to elaborate . . .

I deleted words I wanted to keep.

260

This is a reality for line-editing. I had to delete some of my more creative descriptions. One of the things I loved about Lissa was that she didn't just tell me to delete them. She explained why they weren't working.

Descriptions shouldn't pull the reader from the story. Not even for the sake of admiring the prose. We can get away with it on occasion, but the more often we do it, the more we risk creating a choppy read for our audience. And choppy's never good.

I'm learning that subtle and simple is usually best. A hard lesson for a writer who tends to go purple.

My voice is still my voice.

Lissa suggested changes, and even made changes, but she did so in my voice. She stayed true to who I am on the page and put to rest my biggest fear: That by the time this story makes it to the shelf, it will no longer sound like me.

Line-editing is painful.

Yes, it is. But not for the reasons I expected.

Deleting a beloved description wasn't the painful part.

Having to scrutinize a novel I didn't want to scrutinize was.

I had to look at so many of my words and make sure they meant what I wanted them to say. I had to look at so many of my details and make sure they were accurate and well-researched.

And I had to do it all while wanting to chuck the story out the window. At this point, I've edited this thing more times than I can count.

Combing through it so meticulously yet again made me cross-eyed. My lovely editor, Shannon Marchese, assured me that my strong feelings of dislike toward my story were very normal.

The pain is worth it.

Saying goodbye to some of my words was hard. But after stepping back, I discovered that Lissa was usually right. The changes improved the story. And although I might be permanently cross-eyed, it's now much cleaner. Much smoother. Much better.

I'm learning something I always suspected. Editors are amazing. At least the good ones are.

And when it comes to editing, we're wise to ignore those feelings of defensiveness, embrace some humility, and trust that they know what they're doing.

Chances are, they've been doing it a lot longer than we have.

NINETY

Lessons I Learned from My Editor

Kariss Lynch

From conception to finish, I spent a couple of years on my first novel, *Shaken.* I had a mentor who coached me, a professor who professionally edited the manuscript, and an internationally acclaimed novelist who provided a critique. But nothing affected my story quite as much as signing with my publisher and beginning work with my editor.

Writing is difficult. You are bleeding your emotional artery on the page, complete with life experiences, beliefs, and creativity. But editing? That became another playing field entirely. In my military-romance-driven brain, it could be described as surgery to remove shrapnel. Each piece of metal must be plucked for an individual to get back to full health. In a similar way, editing requires painful digging to remove everything that does not add value to the character. After the shrapnel of your story is removed, you are freed to enhance and improve your story until it's as close to perfection as you can get it this side of heaven.

Working with an editor is refining, a true process of iron sharpening iron (just don't throw the sword at them if you don't like what they say), but ultimately, it is a beautiful journey. The longer I work with my editor, the more I am thankful that God gifted her to look at stories differently than I do. She makes me better, and she is constantly teaching me and reminding me of craft tips that just haven't taken root yet. Over the course of writing *The Heart of a Warrior* series, here is what my editor has taught me:

<u>Timeline is everything.</u>

By the time my first novel went to my editor, the timeline needed major surgery, something I hadn't thought about in great detail during crafting. I am a pantser and only use a bullet point outline to guide the major points of my scenes. Everything else just spills out on the page. This can make editing much harder for me. When it came time to edit *Shadowed*, I had a better time-line in place. Lesson learned? Don't make the same mistakes on the second novel as you did on the first.

<u>Ground your character. Ground your scene.</u>

Ever heard of floating head syndrome? No? Well, that's probably because I just made it up. But I have it. Bad. Especially when I am writing in a steady stream of consciousness. Characters speak but you don't know what they look like or what is going on around them. Thankfully, I am now aware of this ailment and am working to correct it before the manuscript goes to my editor. Each character needs to be firmly grounded in whatever is going on, each person in the scene accounted for, even if only briefly. Your scene also needs to be grounded within the larger story. Your reader should have no question where the character is, what is going on, who the character is with, and what drama is unfolding.

<u>Provide concrete details. Paint the canvas.</u>

I actually love this part of writing, but I also struggle with fear. What if people think that a place or person doesn't look that way? What if I get a detail wrong? What if, what if, what if? The "what if" game keeps me paralyzed from simply using my imagination and the beautiful tools of my eyes and the Internet to ground a scene exactly as I see it. I use research to make sure I didn't get a basic detail wrong, but otherwise, I craft exactly what I want the reader to see. They are less likely to question what I paint in great detail than they are a canvas where I leave glaring holes due to my own people-pleasing and insecurity. No fear. Write boldly. Paint that canvas, and give the readers a scene they don't have to try to imagine. Let it unfold in all of its beautiful detail. And then make that process even better in the next book.

NINETY-ONE

Self-Editing Tips: Purpose

Barbara Scott

In this post, let's concentrate on an aspect of self-editing that writers rarely hear much about: purpose.

Merriam-Webster's Collegiate Dictionary defines purpose as "(1) something set up as an object or end to be attained: intention; (2) a subject under discussion or an action in course of execution."

The definition of purpose also includes resolution and determination, but for our purposes, we can examine the synonyms for purpose and determine how we might find that important concept in a piece of writing, whether fiction or nonfiction. Synonyms: intent, goal, motive, design, aim, end, objective.

Once you finish your first or second draft, ask yourself, "Did I fulfill my overall purpose for writing this piece, and did I achieve my goal(s) in every scene or section?"

Whoa! That sounds like a tall order, doesn't it? You might be thinking, how long am I supposed to spend on an edit? The answer: as long as it takes. Because if you have not fulfilled your purpose in writing your book, then how can your reader know what you were trying to say?

Let me make this a little simpler by starting with a chapter or even a part of a chapter. Did you intend to make your character unsympathetic in this scene? If not, then you have not communicated the soul of your character to the reader. You have not fulfilled the purpose of that character. The reader might even think, "Marsha would never say that. Why is she being so rude?"

On a greater scale, your story or your nonfiction book should have an over-arching aim or goal—purpose. It is the road that connects you to the reader and pulls the story along. Yes, even a nonfiction book is more successful if it tells a story that persuades your reader to believe in what you're writing about.

Your road will twist and turn in a novel, but you, as the author, should always keep the goal in mind. You don't want to tell your reader up-front what your purpose is, but *you* should know where you're headed. If you take readers down a rabbit trail and nothing of significance happens, they will soon stop following you through the brush and weeds.

Only you know what you want to achieve in your book. If you're leading your reader down a "road less traveled," the trip may be leisurely or it may zip along. You may travel on a super highway, on a country lane filled with potholes, or you may walk with your reader down a garden path.

But if you veer off that highway/road/path just because you have a sudden inspiration, your book may be filled with pointless arguments (nonfiction) or characters who pop out of nowhere to deliver a useless piece of dialogue (fiction).

My purpose in this post is not to say that plotters are better writers than pantsters. You can write your book as you please, but if you know your beginning and where you aim to end—your purpose, your goal, your objective—then the journey will be that much sweeter.

NINETY-TWO

Three Ways to Focus on Editing for the Web

Karen Jordan

Real writing begins with re-writing.
—James A. Michener

I began blogging in 2008, and I've visited many websites to determine the most effective way to communicate online. I developed a helpful web-editing checklist below from my research for a writing workshop using three photographic terms—the panoramic, macroscopic, and microscopic viewpoints.

Panoramic View. Begin the editing process by determining the overall, or broader view, of contents and evaluating your audience, purpose, context, and the design elements.

- Read aloud from the reader's perspective (not the writer's).
- Find main point and sub-points. Can you summarize your piece easily?
- Examine benefits for reader (take-away value).
- Use appropriate fonts (not fancy or distracting to your content).
- Use subheading in boldface type to introduce more points.

Macroscopic View. Take a closer look at paragraphs, word usage, and tone.

- Place main topics near beginning of each paragraph and sentence.
- Limit each paragraph to one main idea.
- Use shorter units of text with more breaks.
- Use an introduction for a "teaser" paragraph (preview for content).
- Avoid long texts that break content into several pages.
- Provide a brief summary or table of contents hyperlinked to each section for text over 500 words. Use lists, hyperlinks, and extra white space for a long document to break up dense patterns of text.
- Avoid slang, jargon, and inappropriate humor.
- Use nondiscriminatory language (e.g., bias based on gender, race, ethnicity, religion, age, sexuality, disability).
- Use common words (appropriate for target audience).
- Avoid vague words.
- Use key words to describe the site in the first 50 words of text.
- Build verbal bridges to connect text (transition).
- Use action verbs rather than passive.
- Incorporate single links into content (embedded into the text).
- Make short, bulleted lists of links.
- Use "Find Out More" links, when details are needed.

Microscopic View. Zoom in on the elements of grammar, mechanics, and punctuation.

- Use the Purdue Online Writing Lab (http://owl.english.purdue.edu) or another style guide to drill down into each of these elements.

Self-editing should distance you from your piece, so you can examine it without the emotional attachment. You can see your actual words, rather than just intentions. Consider these final ideas to help you edit for the web.

- Create style sheet/guide with some common problems, to avoid repetitive research of the editing rules (e.g., grammar, mechanics).
- Find someone to read and edit your work (e.g., critique group, another writer).

Remember: "You write to discover what you want to say. You rewrite to discover what you have said and then rewrite to make it clear to other people" (Donald Murray).

NINETY-THREE

When to Tell Your Inner Editor to Shut Up!

Melissa K. Norris

W e're not supposed to tell people to shut up. We're supposed to be polite and considerate.

I'm here to tell you that sometimes we need to tell our inner editor to shut up.

I'm not saying we don't need to edit our work. On the contrary (see my previous post in this section, "Seven Tips for Self-Editing"), but there is a time and a place for said editing.

When you're writing your first draft, I strongly advise you not to edit. Let your ideas flow. If you try to edit now, you may never finish your novel. Or worse yet, you'll stifle your creativity.

There is another voice, one that may or not be your inner editor. The one that tells you this isn't any good. Why on earth did you think you could be a writer? You should just give up before anyone discovers you can't really write.

These, my friends, are the voice of the enemy. Do not believe his lies.

Recently, I heard these words burn through my mind. When you begin to hear the lies, turn to our source of truth. Pray that God's voice would be the only one you would hear. Ask Jesus to silence everything that is not from Him.

I've started doing this every time I sit down to write. It is making a huge difference. We can choose to listen and believe the voice of truth.

If you're trying to write your first novel or first draft of a new project, focus on getting it all out on paper or the computer screen. It's fine to check and make sure your book is keeping in check with your outline and overall story and character goal, but don't try to make it perfect.

VIII.

Pitching Your Work

NINETY-FOUR

Mastering the Essential Query Letter for Writers

Anita Agers-Brooks

I finally read the book *Outliers: The Story of Success* by Malcolm Gladwell. As I devoured the first few chapters, I thought about my quest as a professional writer. And my impatience in the early days. I wrote about it on my personal blog (www.anitabrooks.com) back in 2009.

But reading Gladwell's research, I realized that even in 2009, I was well on my way to achieving my goals. I simply needed to take every necessary step.

According to studies cited in *Outliers*, it takes an average of 10,000 hours to master anything. I figure it took approximately five years of incessant practice, posts, and projects for me to near the 10,000-hour mark. Although I haven't mastered the art, I'm certainly much better than I was six years ago.

And one of the most critical areas of improvement comes in my creation of query letters. Let's face it, if you can't write a strong query, you won't arrest the attention of any agent, editor, or publisher. Early on, I spent a lot of time studying and honing the elements of this crucial piece.

1. Research

Who specifically should you address your inquiry to? Name. Title.

Where should you send your query? Do they accept email only? Content as an attachment, or in the body of your email? Are they snail mail lovers? Do you have the correct address?

What are they looking for? Does your topic or slant match their needs? Have you formatted your submission according to their guidelines?

When are they accepting submissions, and do they have themes tied to calendars?

Why did you choose them? Did you read something that made you think you would connect? Are you familiar with their needs and believe your work can support them in their mission? If possible, find a common bond or at least prove you've studied what's important to them.

How do they want queries packaged? Some prefer a simple one-page letter, clearly stating your concept as it fits within their guidelines. If interested, they'll ask for a proposal or manuscript later. Others request a proposal or manuscript at the same time you send the letter. Make sure you know what the person you are querying prefers.

2. Hook

No matter how well you've written your article or book content, without something to snatch the reader out of their doldrums on the average of the first seven seconds, your work will go no further. Ask that stirring question to make them think. Make a bold statement that flies in the face of an old cliché. Provide a heart-wrenching statistic, forcing them out of the skin of self. Make their belly shake with laughter.

3. Double Check

Once you've written what you believe is a strong query letter, I suggest you run it through the *Writer's Digest Do's and Don'ts of*

Writing a Query Letter by Brian Klems (find it at www.writersdi-gest.com). This brief but powerful list will show you how to write a query letter in the most effective way possible. Also have someone who knows something about professional writing read it.

A family member, or even a high school English teacher, is not going to provide the insights you need when it comes to publishing in the real world. As long as it's a short, one-time read, many professional writers are willing to do this for someone else who's starting out. We remember those days. Just respect their time, and if one writer can't help, try someone else.

10,000 hours sounds like forever when you are starting out as a writer. But with patient and consistent practice, this important landmark will arrive faster than you think. Start small. Master the query letter first. Then one day, you'll have the honor of mentoring someone else.

NINETY-FIVE

Ten Tips for Writing an Effective Query Letter

Margot Starbuck

Whether you're pitching an article or submitting a book proposal, your query letter—or your cover letter—needs to convince a publisher to keep reading. As you're writing, remember that the reader will be tempted to check out and check Facebook. It's your job to grab and keep a reader's attention!

1. An effective query letter is concise.

Demonstrate you're an effective communicator with the efficient use of words. (1 page!)

2. An effective query letter states your intention.

Be clear, up front, whether you're pitching an article or looking for a publisher.

3. An effective query letter is personal.

Address your letter to a particular person. Has he or she represented or published something similar to your project? Make a meaningful connection with the recipient.

4. An effective query letter clearly identifies your premise.

What is the *one thing* this book or article aims to do? Clearly identify the singular unifying thesis.

5. An effective query letter identifies a reader's felt need.

Why should this be published? What need does it meet? Who has this need? How will reader be helped?

6. An effective query letter captures and holds a reader's attention.

Hook reader's attention with colorful anecdote. Then, work to keep it.

7. An effective query letter communicates your competence.

Highlight the elements of your bio or resume most relevant to this project.

8. An effective query letter pulses with your passion.

Demonstrate your enthusiasm for this project.

9. An effective query letter balances confidence with humility.

Thank the reader for her/his time and offer your availability to discuss project further. Demonstrate humility and teachability.

10. An effective query letter is error-free.

It's one page. Be fastidious.

NINETY-SIX

Pitch Your Book Like It's a Movie (The One-Sentence Synopsis)

Kimberly Vargas

I recently attended a screenplay writing seminar with Publishers and Writers of San Diego. It was taught by writing coach Marni Freedman (www.thewriterinyou.com) and focused on taking an existing book and developing it into a screenplay. Screenplays are extremely concise—they average around one hundred pages. Being concise means really having to know the infrastructure and outline of a story. There are several aspects of screenwriting that are helpful in book writing, and one of those aspects is the creation of a logline.

A logline is a one-sentence synopsis of your story. It is like the cover of a book. A good one makes you want to open it immediately to see what is inside. Before you can create a logline, you will need to understand where your book is going. When you try and select a movie on cable, you see loglines all the time. They are very brief descriptions of the show's content.

For example, let's look at a logline for *The Godfather* by Mario Puzo: *A 1940s New York mafia family struggles to protect their empire from rival families as the leadership switches from the father to his youngest son.* Although *The Godfather* is an epic, the plot can still be boiled down into a one-sentence pitch. Audiences have short attention spans and you only get one chance to make a first impression. Effective loglines are compelling: they draw people in and make them want to know more.

Ready to create your own logline? It can be comprised more easily if you are able to supply the following story formula that Marni will be publishing in an upcoming book—*7 Steps to a First Draft*:

Story idea: Who – Unique Problem – Goal – Ending (Marni Freedman 2010).

Who do you want to write about? Why are they interesting? Why should we care about them and want to follow them?

What unique problem does this person face?

What is this person's goal? How will the person solve it? Who or what will try to stop them?

How does their journey end?

Marni encouraged our group to create loglines, as they are not just for the authors to be able to quickly explain the heart of their story, but also serve as a pitch that can be used when interacting with agents, entering contests, meeting with producers, or anyone with whom you want to engage. If you would like to practice this exercise, think about one of your favorite stories (which can be the form of a book or movie) and create a one-sentence synopsis of the plot and action.

The Lion, The Witch and The Wardrobe: Four children travel to the magical land of Narnia where they must battle an evil queen with the direction of the Lion, Aslan.

Citizen Kane: Following the death of a publishing tycoon, news reporters scramble to discover the meaning of his final utterance.

Toy Story: A cowboy doll is profoundly threatened and jealous when a new spaceman figure supplants him as top toy in a boy's room.

The creation of a logline takes time and effort. It's hard to boil down your story to a one-sentence synopsis. It may take you several attempts, so don't beat yourself up if you find it a harder process than you originally anticipated. You will know that you have stumbled on your perfect logline because it is fun to pitch and rolls off your tongue. Try it out on your friends and watch their reactions. If their eyes light up and they say, "Yeah!" then you know you are on the right track. Just start giving it a shot, and you may find that you understand your story with surprising clarity.

NINETY-SEVEN

The Dreaded Synopsis

Michelle Griep

A synopsis is a cold thing. You do it with the front of your mind.
—J.B. Priestley

Is it only me, or do you break out in a cold sweat just thinking about having to write a synopsis? I can write novels. I can write devotionals. I can even whip out a mean shopping list. But writing the dreaded synopsis brings out the idiot in me. Perhaps, indeed, I have lost the front half of my brain somewhere along the way.

So what's my problem? Am I giving this too much importance? Am I trying to fit in too much information? Has there not been enough dark chocolate in my diet of late?

Regardless, there's no getting around the fact that every writer must construct a synopsis in order to sell a manuscript. Think of it as the bones of your story, or if you like, the short story version of your novel.

3 WAYS TO WRANGLE A PLOT INTO A SYNOPSIS FORMAT

1. Introduce your main characters, focusing most on goals, motivations, and conflicts rather than on physical attributes.

Hint: Think back cover copy.

Example: It takes a thief to catch one, and there's none better than reformed cat burglar (MOTIVATION) Officer Doug Harwell. He'll stop at nothing to rid the Boston streets of crime (GOAL)—until the beautiful pickpocket Rhianna Davis enters his life (CONFLICT).

2. For the body of the synopsis, set up each paragraph with the actions, reactions, and decisions made by those main characters.

Example: Bob kisses Donna under the apple tree (ACTION).

He makes her forget she's already engaged to Bubba (REACTION).

Donna decides to break off her engagement and run away to join the circus instead (DECISION).

3. Tie up the loose ends.

Never—ever—leave an editor guessing, no matter how cute you think it is. Cliffhangers are great for chapter endings, but not for a synopsis finale. You must include the resolution to your story.

There you have it. Put together your story idea into a two-page format before you dig into chapter one so that you have a road map to follow as you compose.

DO NOT LIVE AND DIE ON SYNOPSIS HILL

Are you prepared for the zombie apocalypse? I'm not. Shoot, I'm not even prepared to make dinner tonight. I've got more important things on my mind, like should I stick to my synopsis or deviate in a whole new direction even though I'm two-thirds of the way finished? Don't smirk. This is a serious crisis.

What do you do when you suspect your storyline might be one of the living dead?

First off, don't panic. I never do. Oh, I did on the first three or four manuscripts, but now I see a pattern. I get bored with my own story. Yeah, I said that out loud. And newsflash: If the author's bored, the reader will be bored. It's a valid reason to stray from your original outline, but there are a few other reasons you might want to consider when deciding if you should revamp your plan or ditch it altogether.

You might want to change your synopsis if:

1. You thought of a better idea for an ending.

2. A new character shows up and takes center stage.

3. You realized an angle to turn the story into a series.

4. You came across information that makes your original idea not only implausible but outright impossible.

Remember, a synopsis written before a story is finished is more of a *guideline than a legal contract*. It's okay to change things up, unless you've already got a contract on the piece. Then you'll have to clear it with an editor first.

NINETY-EIGHT

Want to Get Published?
Three Things a Publisher Must See

Margot Starbuck

You have a book in your heart that you'd love to see published. It may even be a great book. A publisher and her editing board need to see three things to say the "yes" you're hoping for. They need to see: a unique project, a viable market and the right author.

1. A Publisher Needs to See a Unique *Project*

Although what you're writing may seem fresh to you, know that publishers have already received countless pitches for "My Cancer Journey," "My Eating Disorder Journey," "My Spiritual Memoir." Does this mean you scrap your project? No. But it does mean that you need to demonstrate how yours is unique. For example, these might catch a publisher's attention:

- Why Cancer Was the Best Thing to Happen to Me This Year
- How My Eating Disorder Was Cured When I Won "The Biggest Loser"
- I Was a Satanist High Priest and Now I Love Jesus

Make an editor curious enough to open your proposal!

One baby step toward publication: Read other books in your genre and identify what, if anything, makes yours unique.

2. A Publisher Needs to See a Viable *Market*

The publisher also needs to see that there is a market for this book. Who are the readers who will buy your book? What is the felt-need they have that will cause them to purchase your book, read it and rave about it to their friends? Research the market so that you can demonstrate that there are book-buying readers who need your book.

One baby step toward publication: Develop a one- or two-sentence "elevator pitch" that succinctly communicates the substance of your book, who will read it and what distinguishes it from similar books.

3. A Publisher Needs to See an *Author* Who Can Write and Promote This Book

A publisher is looking for authors who can write and who can also get that writing before an audience.

You've probably heard that author platform—your ability to reach readers—is the most important thing to a publisher. (And it's pretty important.) But hear this: *every publisher wants to publish great writing.*

Chapters and pages and paragraphs and sentences and phrases need to engage readers. Your goal is to get a publisher (aka "reader") to read the first sentence of your proposal and want to read the next one and the next one. You may think it's an editor's job to give your proposal a thorough reading, but it's not. Her *job* is to find quality books to publish. When she is perusing your proposal, she can check out—and check Facebook—at any point in the process. Develop your craft so that you can write prose that a reader does not want to put down.

And there's also that platform business . . .

Who has platform? Oprah. Rick Warren. Francis Chan.

Intimidated? You don't need to be. You can be building your platform right now by:

- pitching and writing articles for publications
- developing an audience for your blog
- building your speaking resume by speaking places for free: MOPs groups, churches, etc.

The key is finding what works for you and sticking with it.

One baby step toward becoming a great writer: Sign up for a local writing class, sometimes available at city colleges, or attend a writer's conference in your area.

One baby step toward building platform: Set a goal to publish one article or story, with a reputable national publication that appeals to the eventual audience for your book, in the next three months.

NINETY-NINE

Five Ways to Break Up a Writing Iceberg: The Book Proposal

Gillian Marchenko

I remember the day well.

After four years, hours and hours of writing, time away from my kids, countless books read on craft, writing classes, and two professional edits, I finally finished my 260-page memoir.

"Success is a finished book, a stack of pages each of which is filled with words. If you reach that point, you have won a victory over yourself no less impressive than sailing single-handed around the world.'—Tom Clancy

Mr. Clancy's quote, once my eyes stumbled upon it, coaxed a satisfied sigh from my gut. I closed my eyes, imagining myself at the helm of a ship, arms stretched out like Rose and Jack from *The Titanic.*

But seriously, *like the next day,* my excitement and feelings of great accomplishment hit an iceberg when I forced myself to pay attention to two words that had floated around my mind throughout the project:

BOOK PROPOSAL.

If my manuscript is the *Titanic,* then the book proposal is the iceberg.

A book proposal is a thorough description of a manuscript, the market it would serve, and a sample of the story, usually the first two or three chapters.

And something I had no idea about until my manuscript was nearly completed.

Once my manuscript was finished, I assumed I could change the sail on my writing ship, pound out a quick proposal, and venture into new waters of querying agents.

Not so.

I had no idea about the painstaking amount of work a thorough, well-written, well-representing book proposal entailed. It took time and several confusing revisions to write an acceptable book proposal.

So here's some advice, sailor to sailor:

1) **Discern the genre**. Book proposals, and when to submit them, are different depending on fiction or nonfiction. Fiction and memoir manuscripts should be completed before the proposal is submitted to an agent or a publisher. Nonfiction books can and do sell on proposal with a couple of chapters to provide the flavor and quality of the writing.

2) **Work on your proposal while you are writing your manuscript.** I should have started researching book proposals right away. Writing the proposal while working on the manuscript would have provided needed focus. A proposal can be a great map of where you are in your project, and where you need to go.

3) **Write well.** Your book proposal is probably the first writing sample a prospective agent or editor will see from you. Don't rush. Let the voice rendered in your manuscript seep onto the proposal page. Agents and editors see many proposals. Take

the time and attention required to make your proposal flawless and flavorful.

4) **Stick to the basic elements of a proposal.** Some include a cover page, an overview of the story, the hook, a biography of the author, marketing strategies, chapter summaries, and sample chapters.

I purchased a template from a famous author. It was a great way to get me started, but once an agent was landed, she preferred I use her agency's template. Though similar, it wasn't quite the same. Realize that an agent or editor will probably want you to tweak your proposal.

5) **A successful book proposal requires research.** Learn from the best. Check out:

Book Proposals That Sell: 21 SECRETS TO SPEED YOUR SUCCESS by Terry Whalin

Writing a Winning Book Proposal by Michael Hyatt

Write the Perfect Book Proposal by Jeff Herman

How to Write a Book Proposal by Rachelle Gardner

How Writing a Proposal Is a Lot Like Teething

Sarah Joy Freese

W e've hit the teething stage at our house which means a lot of crying/whining (especially at 2:05 a.m.), drooling, and biting. I still haven't figured out how Baby Boy manages to fit almost his entire fist into his mouth. I have, however, made a lot of comparisons of teething to the writing process, specifically to proposal writing.

1. **It's painful.** Have you ever seen the show *So You Think You Can Dance*? Each week certain contestants who are in the bottom after the voting process have to dance for their life. They are allowed to dance in their style, but they must pour their heart and soul into their dance to prove to the judges that they still deserve to be in the competition. Similarly, think of your proposal as writing for your life. It is the first major part of your writing (after the initial query) that an agent sees. It is also what gets sent out to editors. If it is written well enough and an agent doesn't have to do much editing, that enhances your chances of landing an agent. Therefore, writing a proposal should be painful. Pour your heart and soul into it. Create the best proposal possible. Razzle dazzle your audience–show them you can write.

2. **Writing a proposal includes a lot of crying/whining (especially at 2:05 a.m.).** Agonize over the proposal. Research

291

how to write a strong proposal. Don't just find the first one that you like and copy it. View several of your favorites and compare them, looking to see what they all include. Spend time on the proposal. Just like you spent time writing and editing your manuscript, you should also spend time writing and editing your proposal.

3. **Sometimes you have to bite (on chocolate) to help you through the pain.** Use whatever inspires you to write a strong proposal. Get in the writing zone. Although a proposal isn't as creative as novel writing, to write a good proposal, you need to be in the creative zone. An agent and an editor can tell a well-written proposal verses one that is written because you have to. So, go for a walk or a run to 'shake your sillies out,' grab some chocolate and some coffee, and sit down to write. As an example, right now I am writing outside on my balcony viewing a beautiful moon—it has that 'man in the moon' look, and tonight it seems as if he is whistling. The neighbors are playing country music (which I love), and I can hear crickets and the wind brushing the leaves of the trees. I am in writing heaven. Now, if a bug flies in my hair, I am going back inside to my living room couch.

What exactly should you include in a proposal? Again, there are several blogs and websites out there that teach what to include in a good proposal, but here are just a few tips to remember.

1. **Platform, platform, platform (even if you write novels).** Have you hit a dry spell in your novel? Consider writing a short story and pitch it to literary journals (both in print or online). If you're a nonfiction writer, write and pitch to magazines or journals that print your subject matter. Get your name out there. Any publication is something you can include on your

proposal. Connect on social media. See if you can book speaking gigs, even if it is just ten people at a local Bible study. Connect widely, but also connect deeply, especially with influencers.

2. **Pretty prose (but not purple).** Engage your readers with your writing. What can you do to make your proposal stand out above the others? How can you add your own style and flare? Obviously there are certain sections that need to be pretty straightforward, but there are others that lend themselves for your own personality to shine through. Start with your biography. How can you show agents and editors who you are not just by listing your credentials?

3. **Polished.** Consider bringing your proposal to your critique group. Have an editor read through for grammar/mechanics errors. Edit, edit, edit. Don't just edit it once, twice, or even three times. Edit it thirteen times. Or eighteen. And have your critique partners do the same.

Making Eye Contact

Dianne Christner

I survived the hottest recorded day in Phoenix—122 degrees, June of 1990.

Slogan tee-shirts celebrated our feat of endurance and brought camaraderie to Phoenicians. Strangers on the street—if we were crazy enough to be outside that particular June—shook heads and bonded without muttering a word. Normally in metropolitan Phoenix, people don't make eye contact with strangers. But survivors bond.

On writing island, the heat's rising and the competition's growing.

Passivity kills. We must seize all survival tools to inhabit, flourish, and keep our cool. There's a handy item in the writer's backpack that can catch the eye of tribal leaders.

A Killer Book Proposal!

I hear your groans. I groaned when the mercury hit 122.

But book proposals create eye contact with your agent or editor.

If you need a format, here's a simplified version of the one from my backpack.

Title Page: Title, author's name, and literary agent's contact information.

Proposal Overview: This vital area creates initial eye contact. It's the premise for a book or series. Be precise. One to two sentences for each book.

Synopsis: Deepen interest. About three pages of story summary (my most recent included a twist and a takeaway). After that, do a three-quarter-page synopsis for each sequel. Note how the books tie together. (For nonfiction proposals, this area contains chapter outline and short summaries).

Manuscript Details: Word count and date when the finished manuscripts can be available (first time authors need to have the manuscript completed, if it's fiction).

Author's Uniqueness: One page. Includes education, credentials, awards, and personal experiences *which relate to your book*, your writing style as compared to others, and genre. If you're published, bring in quotes and snippets of reviews *to describe your writing*.

Marketing: Bullet style, brainstorm what will sell the book. If you write romance, are there some romantic elements that will appeal to readers? Mention them. Tell what you're already doing to promote your platform or books. Explain what you're willing to do. List your website and blog links. Talk about your social media outreach. List memberships and organizations.

Affinity Groups: Research what specific groups of people will read your book. If you have previous works, this is easier. You can even use Facebook or website tracking to pinpoint the age of followers. Being specific helps editors promote your idea to an acquisitions committee.

Books Under Contract (or) Previous Works: Before I had books published, I listed magazine articles and plays. In my last proposal, I only listed a series under contract because it gave a fresh representation of my readership. Include sales in units and earnings. You can get this from your agent or royalty statements.

Author Bio: Mine is about half a page, with professional credentials and some personal information.

First Three Chapters: These significant chapters allow your person of interest to look deep into your writing soul. Shine and represent your style.

On each page, a header contains the book's title and author's name. Single space the proposal and use 1.5 spacing for sample chapters and between headings. My numbered pages usually run about 35 pages total, including sample chapters. Also, write a short summary, about one to three paragraphs, to accompany the cover letter or your agent's email to publishers.

To survive writers' island, proposals can't be rushed. Make the most of the opportunity to create *eye contact*. My format contains years of personal tweaking, but you'll want to embellish whatever format you use with your own creativity and style.

Acknowledgments

This book was created from blogs posts on the WordServe Water Cooler (www.wordservewatercooler.com) by authors from WordServe Literary. There are dozens of authors who contributed to this book, and many more we had to leave out for space considerations. Please read their bios in the back of this book and go to their websites. There are some really fantastic authors you're going to want to become familiar with.

I am grateful to the contributions of Jordyn Redwood, Alice Crider, and Keely Boeving for making the Water Cooler so successful. It's been a Writer's Digest Award Winner for several years. Because of your editorial eye and organizational ability, I can only say, "Great is your reward in heaven." Seriously, you're appreciated far more than I can possibly do in this small space. Thank you for your commitment to great writing and even greater books.

About the Contributors

Anita Agers-Brooks motivates others to dynamic breakthroughs, blending mind, heart, body, and spirit as an Inspirational Business/Life Coach and International Speaker. She shares encouragement on the stage and from the page—reminding audiences, "It's never too late for a fresh start with fresh faith." Anita is also a multi-published, award-winning author. Her titles include Readers' Favorite International Book Award winner: *Getting Through What You Can't Get Over, First Hired, Last Fired — How to Become Irreplaceable in Any Job Market,* and *Death Defied-Life Defined: A Miracle Man's Memoir.* Find out more at www.anitabrooks.com.

Jennie K. Atkins is a manager of two teams of software engineers, one located stateside the other in Mumbai, India. When not at her day job she writes about individuals who discover God's healing grace while struggling to overcome the mistakes of their past. A native Ohioan, Jennie and her husband now live in a small valley east of Carson City, Nevada. They have four children and three grandchildren. Visit her at www.jennieatkins.com.

Rebecca Boschee is the author of two contemporary romances, *Mulligan Girl* and *Last Resort,* from Avalon Books. She has recently expanded her writing voice to include paranormal young adult and is working to build her niche there. Though born and raised in the Midwest, she's lived in Arizona long enough for her blood to have thinned. When not reading, writing, or spending precious time with family, Rebecca enjoys traveling, browsing bookstores and libraries, and visiting the many wonderful spas the Valley has to offer. Find out more at rebeccaboschee.com.

Jeff Calloway is a Missionary Writer devoted to spreading the good news and love of Jesus Christ. He serves as the Send City Missionary with the North American Mission Board in Cleveland, and has established church planter training schools that focus on training and coaching church planters in the Cleveland Metro area. He and his wife Julie have two daughters and three grandchildren. Find out more at www.jeffcalloway.com.

Julie Cantrell is the *New York Times* and *USA Today* bestselling author of *Into the Free*, a debut novel that earned both the Christy Award Book of the Year (2013) and the Mississippi Library Association's Fiction Award. The sequel, *When Mountains Move*, won the 2014 Carol Award for Historical Fiction. Her third novel, *The Feathered Bone*, an Okra Pick by SIBA, released January 2016, earning a starred review by Library Journal. Find out more at www.juliecrantrell.com.

Dianne Christner is a bestselling author who writes light-hearted Christian Fiction. After writing historical fiction for Barbour Books since 1994, she recently penned some Mennonite fiction works. Dianne resides in New River, Arizona, with her husband of forty-four years. They embrace the warm desert lifestyle and enjoy their family—two married children and five grandchildren. She's taught many Sunday School classes and led women's Bible studies. Dianne and Jim attend Desert View Bible Church. Find her at www.diannechristner.net.

Alice Crider is a Senior Acquisitions & Development Editor at David C Cook. During her almost 20 years in publishing, she has worked with a number of bestselling authors, and she teaches writing and editing workshops at writer's conferences nationally and internationally. Also a certified life coach, Alice lives in Colorado, where she enjoys hiking, horseback riding, organic gardening, and spending time with her family.

Megan DiMaria is an author and speaker who enjoys encouraging women to embrace life's demands and delights. She is an active member of several writers groups and is the author of two women's fiction novels, *Searching for Spice* and *Out of Her Hands*. Megan is a social media pro, nonfiction writer, editor, and content creator. She has also been a radio and television reporter. Megan lives in suburban Denver and loves being a wife, mother, and Mimi. You can find her online at www.megandimaria.com.

Jan Drexler brings a unique understanding of Amish traditions and beliefs to her writing. Her ancestors were among the first Amish, Mennonite, and Brethren immigrants to Pennsylvania in the 1700s, and their experiences are the inspiration for her stories. Jan lives in the Black Hills of South Dakota with her husband of more than thirty years, where she enjoys hiking in the Hills and spending time with their four adult children and new son-in-law. Find her at www.jandrexler.com.

Jan Dunlap is the author of *Archangels Book I: Heaven's Gate,* a new Christian suspense novel that melds cutting-edge science with faith. She is also the author of *Saved by Gracie*, her best-selling humorous spiritual memoir, and the Birder Murder Mystery series. When she's not playing with fictional devices, Jan is a birdwatcher, a featured speaker, and the proud mother of five children. She welcomes visitors at jandunlap.com.

Dena Dyer is a wife, mom, speaker, author of eight books, and contributor to many more. She loves encouraging hurting, harried women to find hope and healing in the arms of Jesus...and take themselves less seriously. Her latest book is Love at *First Fight: 52 Story-Based Meditations for Married Couples* (co-written with her husband, Carey). You can find out more about Dena's writing/speaking/mentoring at www.denadyer.com.

Leslie Leyland Fields is the award-winning author of 10 books, including her most recent, *Crossing the Waters: Following Jesus through the Storms, the Fish, the Doubt and the Seas.* She lives in Kodiak, Alaska where she works in commercial fishing with her family and runs the Harvester Island Wilderness Workshop for writers. The rest of the year she travels often to speak around the country on matters of Writing, Faith and Culture. Find her at www.leslieleylandfields.com.

Sarah Joy Freese is a literary agent with WordServe Literary. She loves reading through queries, working with her authors on various proposals, and attending writing conferences to meet new excellent writers. Sarah especially enjoys working with authors to make their manuscripts even stronger. Sarah received her bachelor's degree in English and communications from Cornerstone University in Grand Rapids, Michigan. She also has an MA (emphasis in creative writing) and an MLIS degree from the University of Wisconsin-Milwaukee. Sarah is married and is enjoying life with her husband, sons, and two birds, Brewster and Beamer. Find her at www.wordserveliterary.com.

Katie Ganshert is a slightly frazzled, ever-inquisitive, award-winning author of inspirational fiction. She also writes young adult fiction under the nom de plume K.E. Ganshert. When she's not busy penning novels, she enjoys spending time with her family, drinking coffee with friends, reading great books, and eating copious amounts of chocolate. Find her at katieganshert.com.

Michelle Griep has been writing since she first discovered blank wall space and Crayolas ... professionally, however, for the past 10 years. She resides in the frozen tundra of Minnesota, where she teaches history and writing classes for a local high school co-op. You can find her at: www.michellegriep.com, www.writerofftheleash.blogspot.com, or on Twitter, Facebook, or Pinterest.

Heather Ijames is the author of *Unholy Hunger* and *Hands of Darkness*. Heather is also a practicing attorney and a newspaper columnist. She lives in Nevada with her husband and two children.

Becky Johnson is an author and blogger along with her daughter Rachel at www.welaughwecrywecook.com. Their newest book, an enlightening and humorous journey about self-care, is titled *Nourished: A Search for Health, Happiness and a Full Night's Sleep* (January 2015, Zondervan). They also authored *We Laugh, We Cry, We Cook*, a humorous food memoir, in 2013.

Karen Jordan encourages others to tell the stories that matter most. As an author, speaker, writing instructor, and blogger at karenjordan.net, she focusing on topics about faith, family, and writing. Karen holds an MA in Professional and Technical Writing from the University of Arkansas at Little Rock. A native Texan, Karen and her husband, Dan, live in Hot Springs Village, Arkansas, near their children and grandchildren. Find her at www.jordankaren.com.

Patty Kirk writes spiritual memoir, food memoir, and fiction and is Writer in Residence at John Brown University, where she teaches creative writing. Her most recent book is *The Easy Burden of Pleasing God*. Find her at www.amateurbeliever.com.

Sharon A. Lavy writes inspirational women's fiction. She lives with her husband on a farm in SW Ohio. When not reading, writing, or sewing for her family, Sharon enjoys traveling with her husband in the small plane they named Charley. Find out more at www.sharonalavy.com.

Kariss Lynch writes contemporary fiction about characters with big dreams, hearts for adventure, and enduring hope. She is the author of the Heart of the Warrior series with *Shaken, Shadowed*, and *Surrendered*. Making her home in Dallas, TX, Kariss can usually be found on coffee dates with friends, jamming to country music, or curled up reading a good book. Find her at karisslynch.com.

Gillian Marchenko is the author of *Still Life, A Memoir of Living Fully with Depression* (InterVarsity Press, 2016). Her first book, *Sun Shine Down* (T. S. Poetry Press) about her daughter's birth and diagnosis of Down syndrome in Eastern Europe, released in 2013. She and her husband Sergei spent four years as church planters in Kyiv, Ukraine with the Evangelical Free Church of America and they now live with their four daughters in St. Louis, Missouri. Catch up with Gillian on her author page on Facebook or at gillianmarchenko.com.

Henry McLaughlin, tagged as "one to watch" by *Publishers Weekly,* lives in North Texas where he writes, teaches, and coaches. His stories take readers on adventures into the hearts and souls of his characters as they battle inner conflicts while seeking to bring restoration and justice to a dark world. Visit him at www.henrymclaughlin.org.

Paul (Kent) Muckley hopes to spur interest in the Bible for readers of all ages and backgrounds. He has written several books, including *Know Your Bible: All 66 Books Explained and Applied* (more than 2 million copies sold), *Bible Curiosities, Playing with Purpose: Baseball Devotions,* and *The Real Force: A 4G-Day Devotional.* In his day job, Paul edits books for other writers. He and his wife, Laurie, have adopted three children and live near Grand Rapids, Michigan.

Melissa K. Norris writes inspirational historical romance novels. A skilled artisan crafter, she creates new traditions from old-time customs for her readers. She found her own little house in the big woods, where she lives with her husband and two children in the Cascade Mountains. She writes a monthly column, Pioneering Today, for the local newspaper that bridges her love of the past with its usefulness in modern life. Her most recent book is *The Made-From-Scratch Life.* Find out more at www.melissaknorris.com.

J. Parker is the author of two books on sex in marriage, *Hot, Holy and Humorous,* and a collection of marriage stories, *Behind Closed Doors.* She writes the Hot, Holy & Humorous blog, where she uses a biblical perspective and blunt sense of humor to foster Christian sexuality in marriage. Find out more at hotholyhumorous.com.

Rachel Phifer is the author of the contemporary novel, *The Language of Sparrows*. As the daughter of missionaries, Rachel grew up in four different countries (U.S., Malawi, South Africa and Kenya) and had attended eleven schools by the time she graduated from high school. She holds a BA in English and psychology and now makes her home in Houston with her family. You can visit her website at www.rachelphifer.com or her writing blog at www.novelrenaissance.com.

Dr. Christina M. H. Powell is the author of *Questioning Your Doubts: A Harvard PhD Explores Challenges to Faith*. She is a bioresearch consultant and medical writer who conducted cancer research at the Dana-Farber Cancer Institute and Harvard Medical School. She holds a Ph.D. from Harvard University in Virology, where she studied how viruses can be used as a tool to better understand cancer. She is also an ordained minister with the Assemblies of God. Visit her website at www.christinamhpowell.com.

Jordyn Redwood is a pediatric ER nurse by day, suspense novelist by night. She hosts Redwood's Medical Edge, a blog devoted to helping authors write medically accurate fiction. Her first two medical thrillers, *Proof* and *Poison*, garnered starred reviews from *Library Journal*. *Proof* was shortlisted for the 2012 ForeWord Review's BOTY Award, 2013 INSPY Award and the 2013 Carol Award. *Poison* was shortlisted for the 2014 INSPY Award and the 2014 Selah Award. In addition to her novels, she blogs regularly at Redwood's Medical Edge and the WordServe Water Cooler. You can connect with Jordyn via Facebook, Twitter, Pinterest, her website (www.jordynredwood.com) and via e-mail at jredwood1@gmail.com.

Barbara J. Scott has jumped back into the inspirational waters as an author after taking a fifteen-year hiatus to work as a senior acquisitions editor in the Christian book industry with Zondervan, Abingdon Press, and Honor Books. Her debut novella in the Home Sweet Home contemporary romance Christmas anthology will be released by Gilead Publishing in Fall 2016. She and her husband, Mike, live in the Nashville area where she also edits book manuscripts for other bestselling authors. Find her at barbarajscott.com.

Laurie Polich Short is a speaker, author, and part time pastor of Ocean Hills Covenant Church in Santa Barbara, CA. She speaks at conferences, colleges, churches and denominational events around the country and has spoken to over 500,000 people in the last 25 years. A graduate of Fuller Theological Seminary, Laurie is the author of *Finding Faith in the Dark* (Zondervan 2014). Laurie's next book, *When Changing Nothing Changes Everything*, will be released by IVP in 2017. Laurie lives in Santa Barbara with her husband Jere, and stepson Jordan. Find out more at www.laurieshort.com.

Amy K. Sorrells is a longtime believer in the power of story to change lives. She got her start in journalism and medical writing, and her work has been featured in a wide array of publications including newspapers and medical journals. Her novels have been shortlisted for the 2014 Inspy awards, semi-finalists for the ACFW Genesis awards, and a winner of the 2011 Women of Faith writing contest. An Indianapolis native and graduate of DePauw University, Amy lives with her husband, three sons and a gaggle of golden retrievers in central Indiana. Find her at amyksorrells.com.

Margot Starbuck is an award-winning author and speaker. Margot's first book, *The Girl in the Orange Dress*, was awarded the 2011

Golden Scroll Award for Nonfiction Book of the Year by the Advanced Writers and Speakers Association, and she was a finalist for Selah Awards Best Christian Living Book in 2015 for *Not Who I Imagined.* She also serves as a collaborative writer and ghostwriter, helping others tell their stories. Find her at www.wordmelon.com.

Kimberly Vargas' debut novel, *Gumbeaux,* received a gold medal in the 2011 Readers Favorite fiction contest. Her hobbies are writing, painting, cooking, movies, creative projects, travel and reading. Find her at www.kimberlyvargasauthor.com.

Lisa Velthouse is a freelance writer and speaker. Her latest books are *Craving Grace* (a memoir) and Lauren Scruggs' *Your Beautiful Heart* (for teens.) In her work, Lisa strives to explore and share the reality of that grace. Find Lisa's reflections on faith, family, and military life, plus information about her speaking and books, at www.LisaVelthouse.com.

Erica Vetsch is a transplanted Kansan now residing in Minnesota. She loves history and romance, and is blessed to be able to combine the two by writing historical romances. Whenever she's not immersed in fictional worlds, she's the company bookkeeper for the family lumber business, mother of two, wife to a man who is her total opposite and soul-mate, and avid museum patron. Find her at www.ericavetsch.com.

Janalyn Voigt is a storyteller who brings her unique blend of adventure, romance, suspense, and whimsy to several genres. Beginning with *DawnSinger,* the *Tales of Faeraven* series carries readers into a fantasy land only imagined in dreams. *Deceptive Tide (Islands of Intrigue: San Juans),* a romantic suspense novel, released in June

2016. Look for *Hills of Nevermore* (Montana Gold, book 1), a western historical romance, to release in 2017. Live Write Breathe (www.livewritebreathe.com), the website where Janalyn teaches other writers, was named one of the Write Life's 100 best websites for writers in 2016. Learn more about Janalyn Voigt and her books at www.janlynvoigt.com.

Bob Welch is the author of 21 books, including the Oregon Book Award nominee "American Nightingale," featured on ABC's "Good Morning America." He is a former newspaper columnist, a former adjunct professor of journalism at the University of Oregon and a current writer, speaker and workshop leader. He has twice won the National Society of Newspaper Columnist's "Best Writing" award. He is at bobwelch.net.

The Writing Sisters, Betsy Duffey and Laurie Myers, were born into a writing family, and began critiquing manuscripts at an early age for their mother, Newbery winner Betsy Byars. They went on to become authors of more than thirty-five children's novels written individually and with their mother. When their mother retired they made a decision to use their writing skills to share their faith. Their first book for adults, *The Shepherd's Song*, was published by Simon and Schuster's Howard Books. *The Lord is Their Shepherd: Praying Psalm 23 for Your Children* was released in March 2016. Find them at www.writingsisters.com.

FAITH HAPPENINGS.com

Are you a writer or speaker looking to grow your platform, reach and readership?

FaithHappenings.com can help you do just that!

FaithHappenings.com is an online Christian resource with 454 local websites serving more than 31,000 cities and towns. It offers tailored, faith-enriching content for members. Along with a few dozen other benefits, it connects people of faith to information about books, blogs, speaking events, and other resources that interest them most. As a writer or speaker, it will help you connect with people specifically interested in your genre, subject or brand! So, just what can FaithHappenings.com offer you?

On FaithHappenings.com You Can...

1. For Free... **List yourself as a speaker both locally and regionally**—increasing your visibility in multiple markets

2. For Free... **Announce your book signings** in your area

3. **List your books—both traditionally and self-published** (sent out to members who have requested to hear about new books in your genre)*

4. **Announce special e-book promotions the day they happen** (sent out to members and listed on the site daily!)*

5. **Build your blog traffic** by posting your blog into two categories, and be highlighted as a "Featured Blogger" on our Home Page*

6. **Be a highlighted "Author Interview."** FH Daily runs author interviews several times a week. Just email fhdaily@faithhappenings.com to see if you qualify.

7. **Create more awareness for your book with advertising!** An ad on the site is affordable for any author.*

8. As a free member yourself, you can **receive e-mail announcements for any book** in more than 70 genres

What are you waiting for? Get started today by signing up in your local area to become a member at www.faithhappenings.com.

A small fee applies

ABOUT THE PUBLISHER

FH Publishers is a division of FaithHappenings.com

FaithHappenings.com is the premier, first-of-its kind, online Christian resource that contains an array of valuable local and national faith-based information all in one place. Our mission is "to inform, enrich, inspire and mobilize Christians and churches while enhancing the unity of the local Christian community so they can better serve the needs of the people around them." FaithHappenings.com will be the primary i-Phone, Droid App/Site and website that people with a traditional Trinitarian theology will turn to for national and local information to impact virtually every area of life.

The vision of FaithHappenings.com is to build the vibrancy of the local church with a true "one-stop-resource" of information and events that will enrich the soul, marriage, family, and church life for people of faith. We want people to be touched by God's Kingdom, so they can touch others FOR the Kingdom.

To learn more, visit www.faithhappenings.com.